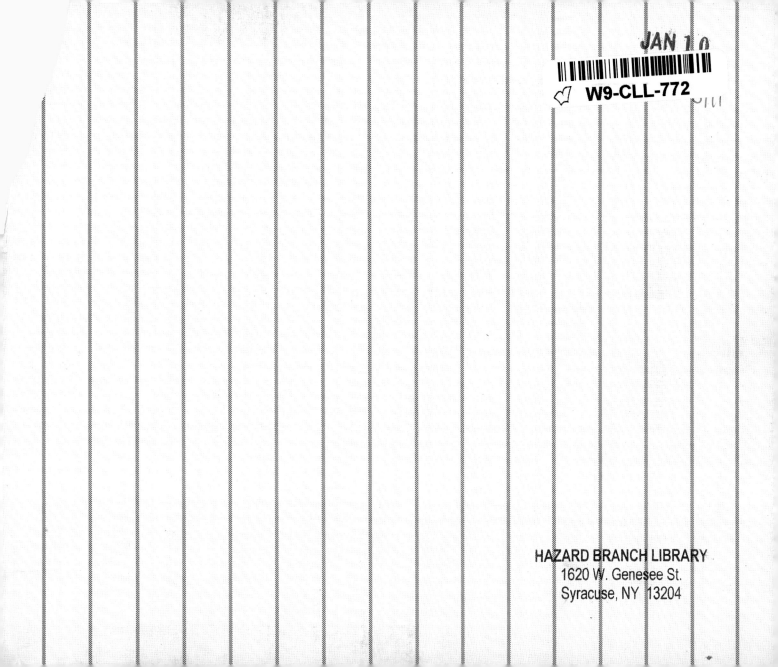

JAN 1 0

W9-CLL-772

For the Love of
the NEW YORK
Yankees

Dave Kaplan

WEST
SIDE
PUBLISHING

Dave Kaplan is director of the Yogi Berra Museum and Learning Center, a nonprofit sports education organization on the campus of Montclair State University in Montclair, New Jersey. Prior to helping found the Museum in 1998, he was an editor and reporter at the Associated Press and the *New York Daily News.* He has also collaborated with Yogi Berra on four books.

Factual verification by **Ken Samelson**

Title page: The Yankee cap has long been a symbol of pride and excellence in baseball.

The brand-name products mentioned in this publication are trademarks or service marks of their respective companies. The mention of any product in this publication does not constitute an endorsement by the respective proprietors of Publications International, Ltd., nor does it constitute an endorsement by any of these companies that their products should be used in the manner represented in this publication.

Front cover: Getty Images (top left); **MLB Photos** (right); **PIL Collection** (bottom left); **Transcendental Graphics** (left center)

Back cover: Getty Images (top); **PIL Collection** (bottom)

AP Images: 8, 18, 23, 27, 42 (right), 46, 59, 74, 80, 93 (right), 112, 120, 134, 138, 152 (right), 156, 161, 163, 166, 172, 174, 177, 181, 182, 189, 199, 204 (left), 217, 219, 221, 232, 234, 235, 246, 254, 256–257, 267, 277, 281; **Compliments of the Candy Wrapper Museum:** 148 (right); **Comstock:** 240; **©Corbis:** Bettmann, 19, 151; **Getty Images:** 8, 20, 47, 50, 55, 57, 67, 72, 79, 82, 88, 92, 95, 97 (left), 99, 103, 117, 121, 128, 139 (left), 147, 153, 171 (right & left), 173, 176, 184, 186, 193, 195, 196 (left), 205, 210 (left), 213, 216, 218, 225, 226, 227, 228, 236, 274, 275, 278, 283; AFP, 5, 44 (left), 129, 142, 145, 214, 215 (right), 251; Diamond Images, 17 (right), 35, 73, 105, 130, 141, 143, 180, 250, 268; Focus on Sport, 68, 126, 139 (right), 159; MLB Photos, 63 (left), 64, 90, 101, 113, 131 (right), 175, 190 (left), 206, 209, 241; *Sports Illustrated,* 231, 233, 284; Time Life Pictures, 106, 152 (left), 243; **Richard Johnson**

Collection: 179, 272, 273; **Library of Congress:** 6; **National Archives and Records Administration:** 25 (top); **National Baseball Hall of Fame Library, Cooperstown, N.Y.:** 8, 22 (right), 32 (right), 36 (left), 37, 40, 71, 83, 98, 107, 111, 114, 116, 132, 144, 162, 187, 220, 222, 224, 229, 248; **PhotoDisc:** 4, 7, 12, 39, 51, 52, 58, 65, 81, 85, 89 (bottom), 93 (left), 94, 96, 110, 131 (left), 170, 223, 245, 266, 269, 279, 280, 285; **Photofest:** 97 (right); **PIL Collection:** 8, 9, 10, 13, 14, 15, 17 (top left & bottom left), 21, 26, 30 (left & right), 32 (left), 36 (right), 41, 44 (right), 45 (left & right), 48, 49, 53, 56, 60, 61, 63 (right), 66, 75, 76, 77, 78, 84, 87, 102, 108, 119, 122, 123, 124, 127 (left & right), 133, 136, 137, 148 (left & center), 149, 155, 158, 164, 178, 190 (right), 191, 192, 194, 196 (right), 197, 198, 200, 201, 202, 204 (right), 208, 210 (right), 211, 215 (left), 244, 249, 252, 261, 264, 265, 276; **Shutterstock:** 109, 115, 118, 125, 135, 150, 152 (bottom), 160, 165, 167, 183, 188, 203, 207, 230, 237, 239, 247, 255, 260, 270, 282; **Transcendental Graphics:** 22 (left), 33; Mark Rucker, 38, 43, 70, 89 (top), 238, 253; Mark Rucker/M. Brown, 62; Mark Rucker/Carwile, 25 (bottom); Mark Rucker/Olenick, 11

West Side Publishing is a division of Publications International, Ltd.

Louis Weber, CEO
Publications International, Ltd.
7373 North Cicero Avenue
Lincolnwood, Illinois 60712

Permission is never granted for commercial purposes.

ISBN-13: 978-1-4127-2933-8
ISBN-10: 1-4127-2933-5

Manufactured in China.

8 7 6 5 4 3 2 1

Library of Congress Control Number: 2008931658

Joe DiMaggio

Whitey Ford

CONTENTS

Lou Gehrig

CHAPTER ONE

MAKING OF THE MYSTIQUE

"It's great to be *young* and a *Yankee.*"

—WAITE HOYT, 1921

IN THE BEGINNING

In 1903, the Wright Brothers' flying machine stayed aloft for 12 seconds. The longest film produced to date, *The Great Train Robbery*, ran 12 minutes. A soft drink called Pepsi-Cola was introduced. And, oh yes, the most powerful and successful franchise in American sports came into existence. Of course, it would take a little time for the team that would eventually be known as the New York Yankees to become powerful and successful.

The team's beginnings were humble, indeed. A high roller named Frank Farrell and former New York City police chief Big Bill Devery paid a paltry $18,000 to buy the former Baltimore franchise and move it to New York to play in the infant American League. Both men had good political connections, which didn't hurt, because New York's other team—the well-established New York Giants—resented having an upstart competitor.

The new team in town needed a place to play. Farrell found a spot in Washington Heights less than a mile northwest of the Polo Grounds, the Giants' home. In six weeks, a modest single-decked wooden structure was built. It seated about 16,000 and was called Hilltop Park, as it was situated on the highest ground of Manhattan. Sitting on West 168th Street and Broadway (now the site of Columbia Presbyterian Hospital), the new ballpark had a grand view of the Hudson River and the Palisades.

Originally, New York's new team was known as the Highlanders, thanks in part to the elevated position of Hilltop Park, but also because the team's new president was Joseph Gordon, and there was a famous British Army regiment known as Gordon's Highlanders. From the start, nobody was really crazy about the name. In addition, the local newspapers found it too long for one-column headlines. Soon, fans began calling the team the Yanks or Yankees, an old slang term for Americans with deep patriotic sentiment.

Led by manager and pitcher Clark Griffith, the team finished in fourth place in its inaugural season. In the following 1904 season, the High-landers—led by 41-game-winning spitball pitcher Jack Chesbro—made a serious run at the pennant. Alas, they lost to the Boston Pilgrims when Chesbro surrendered the winning run on a wild pitch in the bottom of the ninth on the last day of the season.

The presence of the Highlanders in the pennant race prompted the Giants to announce they would not play in the World Series against a "minor league" team. Although Boston had won the pennant, the Giants still refused to partici-pate. Because of the boycott, there was no World Series in 1904.

The Highlanders/Yankees went downhill from there. In 1908, they posted an awful 51–103 record and the owners, Devery and Farrell, were seen squabbling in public. A few years later the owners went broke and sought to sell the club. The new American League team would never come close to winning a pennant again, at least until a big fellow named Babe came along.

Most Iconic Yankees

Babe Ruth
(1920–1934)

Lou Gehrig
(1923–1939)

Joe DiMaggio
(1936–1951)

Yogi Berra
(1946–1963)

Whitey Ford
(1950, 1953–1967)

Mickey Mantle
(1951–1968)

Thurman Munson
(1969–1979)

Don Mattingly
(1982–1995)

Derek Jeter
(1995–present)

Mariano Rivera
(1995–present)

Hal Chase

OFFICIALLY YANKEES

As David Bowie might say, 1913 was a year of ch-ch-changes. The team changed managers, luring former Cubs skipper Frank Chance (of the famed Tinker-to-Evers-to-Chance double play combo) out of retirement. They changed the site of their home field to the Polo Grounds, becoming tenants of the Giants, as Hilltop Park had become woefully outdated. (Fortunately, relations between the Giants and Yankees had improved after Farrell offered the Giants the use of Hilltop Park following a 1911 fire at the Polo Grounds.)

Perhaps the most important change was that they officially switched their name to the Yankees. The nickname had grown in popularity over the team's first decade and with the change in parks in 1913, it no longer made sense to call the team the Highlanders. From then on, the team would be known exclusively as the Yankees.

In another change, the Yankees began their spring training in Bermuda, becoming the first team to train outside the United States. Still, the rum drinks and the official name change didn't do anything to improve their luck. Chance, a legendary tough guy, was convinced that star first baseman Hal Chase was fixing games, and the Yankees finished in seventh place with a 57–94 record.

SECOND-CLASS CITIZENS

When the Yankees moved into the rebuilt Polo Grounds as tenants in 1913, they were hardly considered an attraction. They were dismal, and the Giants already owned the hearts of New Yorkers. Their manager, John McGraw, was a cocky genius, holding sway with his political and theatrical connections. His team also enjoyed supreme glory, winning three straight pennants between 1911 and 1913.

At the time, two wealthy men, Colonel Jacob Ruppert and Captain Tillinghast L'Hommedieu Huston, tried to badger McGraw into selling his team, but the man known as Little Napoleon flatly refused. McGraw instead talked them into buying the Yankees, whose rakish owners Devery and Farrell had gone broke.

So Ruppert, a brewery baron, and Huston, an engineer who made his fortune in Cuba, bought the

Jacob Ruppert

Yankees for $460,000 in 1915. The Colonel and the Captain promptly dedicated themselves to seeing that the Yankees equaled or surpassed the Giants in the affections of New York fans.

That season, the famous Yankee pinstripe uniform became a permanent fixture. Ruppert actually wanted to change the name of the Yankees to the Knickerbockers, after his best-selling beer, but the press balked at the idea. The owners began buying talent, and Ruppert hired a diminutive lawyer named Miller Huggins, who became manager in 1918. Ruppert did this unbeknownst to his partner Huston, who never forgave him for the move. The Yankees shared the Polo Grounds with the Giants for a decade (1913–1922). During that time, the Yankees became respectable, but it wasn't until they moved to their own place that they became invincible.

"*Yankee Stadium* *was a mistake, not mine but the Giants.*"

—YANKEE OWNER JACOB RUPPERT ON
HIS TEAM'S EVICTION FROM THE
POLO GROUNDS

THE STADIUM

Ruppert and Huston searched far and wide for a suitable location to build a new home for the Yankees. They considered Manhattan's West Side and also looked at several sites in Queens. Ultimately, they settled on the 10-acre plot of an old lumberyard in the south Bronx, purchasing it from the estate of William Waldorf Astor for $675,000. Did they ever imagine the spot would be transformed into the most majestic ballpark ever seen?

Thanks to Huston's experience in handling large-scale construction projects, work progressed swiftly. Yankee Stadium was designed by the Osborn Engineering Company to seat approximately 60,000 and was built in only 284 days at a cost of $2.5 million. Today, a team would be lucky to get a utility infielder for that much money.

One striking component of the colossal stadium was the 16-foot-high copper frieze hanging from the roof of the upper grandstand. It became the signature piece for the new ballpark. Adding to the building's character were the quirky field dimensions. Originally, it was a monstrous 490 feet to left-center field, seemingly miles away from home plate. But the right field foul line was only 296 feet, designed to accommodate Babe Ruth's lefty stroke. Field dimensions have changed through the years, but the short right field porch has remained a Yankee Stadium fixture.

The right field bleachers would become known as "Ruthville." In fact, many fans wanted to name the whole ballpark after Babe. Fred Lieb, writing in the *New York Evening Telegram*, first nicknamed the establishment "The House That Ruth Built." Still, Ruppert insisted on calling it Yankee Stadium, and Yankee Stadium it has remained. It was the first ballpark to be called a stadium and the last privately financed ballpark in the major leagues.

When the time finally came to open for business on April 18, 1923, the stadium was a mob scene. The Yankee front office reported more than 74,000 in attendance, many standing in the aisles. Thousands more milled outside the park, turned away from the spectacle.

The inaugural show featured the Yankees versus the Boston Red Sox, with the celebrated march king John Philip Sousa leading both teams onto the field. Governor Alfred E. Smith threw out the first ball. "It is reported on good authority," wrote journalist Heywood Broun, "that when the Babe first walked out to his position and looked about him he was silent for almost a minute while he tried to find adequate words to express his emotions. Finally he emerged from his creative coma and remarked, 'Some ball yard!'"

The Babe had promised he'd do all he could to properly commemorate the stadium's opening. Before the game he said he'd give a year of his life if he could hit a home run in his first game in the new Yankee Stadium. In the third inning, Ruth hit a shot off Howard Ehmke into the right-field bleachers and was greeted with a roar that could be heard all the way over at the Polo Grounds. The Yankees won 4–1, and Yankee Stadium was officially baptized.

Yankee
DOODLE DANDY

When gung-ho Larry MacPhail took over the Yankees in 1945, he was scheming up ideas to lure a war-weary public back to the ballpark. He knew the Yankees had to increase advertising and also that they needed an attractive emblem to put on promotional materials. To connect with the wave of post-war patriotism, Lon Keller, an illustrator, designed a red, white, and blue Uncle Sam hat sitting on top of a bat. Behind both was a baseball emblazoned with the team name. The emblem first appeared in the team's 1947 spring training itinerary and later that year on the cover of the World Series program. More than 60 years later, the Yankees' top hat logo is still a dandy.

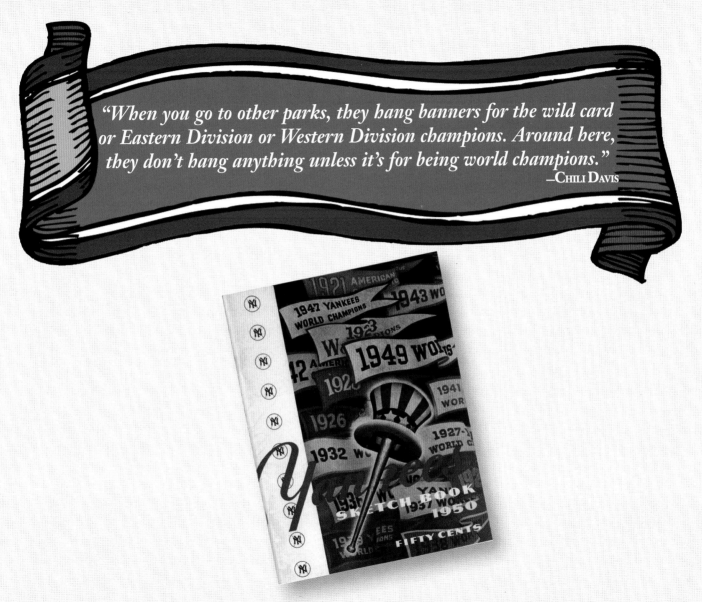

"When you go to other parks, they hang banners for the wild card or Eastern Division or Western Division champions. Around here, they don't hang anything unless it's for being world champions."
—CHILI DAVIS

FRIEZE FRAME

Yankee Stadium—the original and remodeled editions—has always had the short porch in right and the sun field in left. But if there's one distinguishing feature that has given the Stadium its iconic personality, it's the frieze.

For years, the art deco copper frieze (often mistakenly referred to as a facade) adorned the inner roof of the ballpark. The frieze, which was painted white in the 1960s, was 16 feet high and became as integral to Yankee Stadium as the ivy in Wrigley Field or the Green Monster in Fenway Park.

The classic rooftop frieze from 1923 was destroyed in the 1974–1975 renovation. However, it was recast, and the replica framed the outfield bleacher billboards and scoreboard in the remodeled Yankee Stadium (1976–2008). A miniature frieze was also installed over the lockers in the home clubhouse.

For years, the team has used the frieze as a marketing tool on television and in print. Now this symbol of the Yankee tradition from the original "House That Ruth Built" continues in the new Yankee Stadium, which features a 21st-century rendition of the famous frieze.

IS ANYBODY HOME?

One of the low points in Yankee history occurred on September 22, 1966, as the once-proud franchise wallowed in last place. Broadcaster Red Barber asked a WPIX-TV camera operator to scan the more than 66,000 empty seats during an afternoon game against Chicago. "I don't know what the paid attendance is today," Barber said, "but whatever it is it's the smallest crowd in the history of Yankee Stadium, and the smallest crowd is the story, not the ballgame."

Barber, perhaps the most respected and intelligent play-by-play man in baseball history, later found out the paid crowd was 413—and reported it. As a reward for his candor, he was fired by team president Mike Burke.

CLUBHOUSE CONFIDENTIAL

One can't underestimate the magic of the Yankees' clubhouse. It's where the team's chemistry melds and where team leaders emerge. "When Joe [DiMaggio] walked in," legendary trainer Pete Sheehy often said, "the lights flickered."

Best Yankee First Basemen

LOU GEHRIG (1923–1939): Unquestionably the game's greatest at the position

DON MATTINGLY (1982–1995): Had the misfortune of playing in only one postseason during 14 seasons

MOOSE SKOWRON (1954–1962): Clutch performer during '50s glory years

TINO MARTINEZ (1996–2001, 2005): Integral part of late '90s dynasty

CHRIS CHAMBLISS (1974–1979, 1988): Homer to win '76 pennant among the biggest in team history

"*I love playing the*
GAME.
*That's what I'm
here for.*"

—Don Mattingly

PINSTRIPES FOREVER

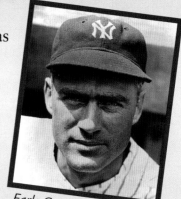

Earle Combs in pinstripes

Pinstripes mean power, and pinstripes symbolize the Yankees. Of course, other teams also wear thin vertical stripes. Some even predate the Yankees in sporting this uniform decoration. The Cubs wore them during the 1907 World Series.

Since the Yankees made pinstripes a permanent feature of their uniforms in 1915, they've become their signature feature, as much as the interlocking NY on their caps.

Legend has it that the Yankees adopted pinstripes to make beer-bellied Babe Ruth look slimmer. This is, of course, a myth, as Ruth did not join the team until 1920.

Truth is, the Yankees first introduced black pinstripes for their home uniforms in 1912, during their last season at Hilltop Park. As *The New York Times* reported on February 27, 1912:

Ruth in pinstripes

"When [manager] Harry Wolverton's Yankees trot out from the clubhouse on April 11 to open the season with Boston, Hilltop fans will see their favorites togged out in uniforms closely resembling those worn by the Giants last year. The fad for the pin stripe in baseball toggery, introduced by the Cubs a few years ago, has reached the Hilltop and the home uniform of the Yankees this year will be of that design . . . ."

The team abandoned the black pinstripes at the end of that season. But in 1915, the classy pinstripes returned, this time in navy blue—and they've never left.

I GOT YOU, BABE

In 1919, the Boston Red Sox were trying to rid themselves of a problem child. George Herman "Babe" Ruth was a carefree, moon-faced pitcher who won a lot of games. He could hit a lick, too, so the Red Sox wisely moved him to the outfield that year. Ruth had no peer as a power hitter, and that season he exploded for 29 homers —a major-league record and a remarkable feat during the dead-ball era. However, Harry Frazee, the Red Sox owner and cash-strapped Broadway producer, felt Ruth's ego and salary demands were too much for his team.

Frazee's distaste for Ruth didn't end there. He also felt that Ruth had already peaked as a player, and worse, Frazee also accused Ruth of being "one of the most selfish and inconsiderate men ever to put on a baseball uniform." Not surprisingly, on January 3, 1920, Frazee announced the sale of the 25-year-old man-child to the Yan-kees for $125,000, with Jacob Ruppert extending Frazee a $350,000 loan, as well.

Miss Manners he wasn't, but Ruth was the game's greatest attraction. That season people flocked to the Polo Grounds to see the Yankees' new barrel-chested, spindly-legged phenomenon. Fans were fascinated by the majestic flight and frequency of Ruth's home runs. In those days, the long ball wasn't such a routine event. Yet Ruth— whose brute power persuaded baseball's powers-that-be to adopt a livelier ball—single-handedly made the home run the premier offensive weapon of modern baseball.

In 1920, Ruth hit .376 with 54 home runs— more than any *team* in the league. Because of Ruth, the Yankees doubled their attendance to almost 1.3 million, becoming the first team to ever top the million mark. Giants' management was hardly enthralled. The team drew 929,000—

a record for them—but they were still peeved by their tenants' rapidly growing popularity. So, in December 1920, the Giants told the Yankees that when their lease expired in two years, they had to leave the Polo Grounds for good.

The Yankees played two more fairly successful years at the Polo Grounds. In 1921, Ruth hit 59 homers and the Yankees won their first pennant, which resulted in the first all-New York World Series and the first to be played entirely in one ballpark. The Giants won that Series and beat the Yankees again in the 1922 Series. Still, the big man, surrounded by a well-balanced cast, had transformed the Yankees. Ruppert planned a three-tier baseball palace across the Harlem River from the Polo Grounds, where Giants management could watch it rise from their executive offices.

Ruppert built the new ballpark to the specifications of his team's biggest star. Babe Ruth could

Ruth signs with Ruppert.

hit a ball over anything, but Ruppert didn't want that to be necessary. The right field fence was built 296 feet away from home plate but was only 43 inches high.

NUMBER NO LONGER IN SERVICE

In 1929, the Yankees became the first team to permanently wear numbers on the backs of their uniforms. Fittingly, they became the first team to retire players' numbers, too. The first number was retired on July 4, 1939, when the Bronx Bombers honored Lou Gehrig—two months after he played his final game—by taking his No. 4 out of circulation.

Babe Ruth was the second Yankee player to have his number retired, but it took a while. Several players wore No. 3 after Ruth left the team in 1935, including George "Twinkletoes" Selkirk and Bud Metheny. In fact, journeyman outfielder Cliff Mapes was wearing No. 3 during Ruth's farewell address at Yankee Stadium on June 13, 1948.

Ruth's number was finally retired after he died in August of that year. Mapes then became the first Yankee player to wear No. 13 and later he wore No. 7, which would later become Mickey Mantle's number.

The Yankees retired No. 8 twice in 1972, for catchers Bill Dickey and Yogi Berra. Ironically, Dickey did not wear this number at the beginning of his career because it was worn by Johnny Grabowski. Nor did he wear it as a Yankee coach; Berra had taken it over.

Babe Ruth's farewell

Yankees Retired Numbers

NUMBER	PLAYER	YEAR RETIRED
1	Billy Martin	1986
3	Babe Ruth	1948
4	Lou Gehrig	1939
5	Joe DiMaggio	1952
7	Mickey Mantle	1969
8	Bill Dickey	1972
8	Yogi Berra	1972
9	Roger Maris	1984
10	Phil Rizzuto	1985
15	Thurman Munson	1979
16	Whitey Ford	1974
23	Don Mattingly	1997
32	Elston Howard	1984
37	Casey Stengel	1970
42*	Jackie Robinson	1997
44	Reggie Jackson	1993
49	Ron Guidry	2003

* Retired throughout MLB

POP QUIZ

1. Which Hall of Famer gave Don Mattingly the nickname "Donnie Baseball"?

2. Who was the last out in Dave Righetti's no-hitter against the Boston Red Sox on July 4, 1983?

3. Why did the Yankees trade spring training sites with the New York Giants in 1951, moving to Phoenix, Arizona, while the Giants took up residence in St. Petersburg, Florida?

4. Who was the oldest Yankee ever to win a Gold Glove?

5. Which Yankee is credited with inventing the batting donut used by players in the on-deck circle?

6. After leaving the Yankees in 1935, Babe Ruth played for what team?

7. Which future Yankee pitcher played baseball in the 1988 Summer Olympics?

8. After a broken bat hit in 1974, what was revealed to be inside Graig Nettles's bat?

1: Kirby Puckett; 2: Wade Boggs; 3: So Yankee co-owner Del Webb could show off his team to his friends in Arizona; 4: Wade Boggs, at 37, in 1993; 5: Elston Howard; 6: Boston Braves; 7: Jim Abbott; 8: Six superballs

NO ORDINARY JOE

Joseph Paul DiMaggio was as incomparable a ball-player as there ever lived. The eighth of nine children of a hardworking Italian immigrant fisher, DiMaggio was never flamboyant, yet was often dramatic. He had an unmatched style and grace and an aura that was unmistakable.

Speaking of mistakes, he seldom made any, physical or mental. DiMaggio was an astounding all-around player. He helped shape the Yankees' championship mystique perhaps more than any other player, Babe Ruth included. He was the epitome of what it meant to be a Yankee.

From the beginning, he was a star. When he joined the team in 1936, he was the most publicized rookie in the history of the game. The Yankees won four consecutive championships in DiMaggio's first four seasons (1936–1939). He was a classic, natural hitter; a fast, smart baserunner; and a smooth, graceful center fielder.

In 1941, he captivated America with his incredible 56-game hitting streak, and he struck out only 13 times all year. He also won the league's MVP award that season despite a landmark performance from Ted Williams, whose .406 average (like DiMaggio's record hit streak) has never been approached since.

After missing three seasons to military service, DiMaggio battled a host of health problems, yet he still managed to perform spectacularly. In 1949, he missed the first two months of the season after heel surgery. In his debut in late June, he pounded four home runs in a three-game sweep of the Red Sox. Battling pneumonia in the last series of the season, DiMaggio still helped lead the Yankees to a pair of victories and the pennant.

In his 13 glorious seasons, DiMaggio won three MVP awards, batted .325 (with a .422 slugging percentage), and racked up 361 home runs, even though, as a right-handed hitter, he was handicapped by the spacious outfield of Yankee Stadium. That didn't matter to him. What mattered was the team, and the Yankees won an amazing nine world championships with DiMaggio in pinstripes.

Though a public hero, DiMaggio was a private man. The great Hank Greenberg once noted that if DiMaggio said hello to you, that was a long conversation. Newspaper columnist Jimmy Cannon, who had known DiMaggio since 1936, once wrote that he was the "shyest public man" he had ever known.

Yet, those who saw him play could never forget his superlative ease and majestic grace. He had earned his stature in the world of baseball and transcended it to become a cultural icon. Long after his career ended, Simon and Garfunkel memorialized him in their song "Mrs. Robinson." In a wistful call to indomitable heroes of the past, they asked, "Where have you gone, Joe DiMaggio? A nation turns its lonely eyes to you."

THE INTERLOCKING NY LOGO

The interlocking NY—the Yankees' world-famous insignia—is one of the oldest, hippest, and most marketable logos in American sports.

More than 130 years after its creation, everyone, from rappers to grandmothers, wears it proudly. It's a symbol of excellence, pride, and class, befitting its origins.

Jeweler Louis Comfort Tiffany, who was son of the founder of Tiffany & Co., designed the logo in 1877. It was presented to the New York Police Department that same year via patrolman John McDowell, who had been shot in the line of duty. Bill Devery, a retired police chief and one of the Yankees' original owners, adopted the logo for his team in 1909.

That year, the Yankees (then known as the Highlanders), put a red-orange, interlocking NY on their black baseball caps. Over the next few years, the Yankees went through a variety of cap designs. By 1922, the Yankees had adopted the now-familiar navy blue cap with a white, interlocking NY logo. In 1936, the Yankees permanently incorporated the NY insignia on the left breast of their home uniforms as well. To this day, the logo has remained unchanged, classic, and cool as ever.

*"**Ruth** is the first and last $80,000 player. The game of baseball does not produce profits permitting the payment of $80,000 to any player. However, even hard-headed businessmen lose their financial judgment when they get into baseball. When I signed Ruth at $80,000, I did so not as a businessman, but as a fan."*

—YANKEE OWNER JACOB RUPPERT AFTER SIGNING BABE RUTH TO BASEBALL'S BIGGEST CONTRACT IN 1930

 # GOLDEN OLDIES

Every year since 1946, the Yankees have staged Old-Timers' Day, a glorious family reunion. Around midseason each year they bring back their former stars and nonstars to again bask in the fans' adulation on the Yankee Stadium diamond. The players all wear Yankee uniforms with their old numbers, are introduced, and even play in a two-inning exhibition.

Old-Timers' Day is more than a bunch of aging ballplayers trying to recapture old glory. It's about nostalgia, camaraderie, and great memories. "Lou Gehrig Appreciation Day" in 1939 might have been the impetus for Old-Timers' Day. For that event, the Yankees brought back the ailing star's old teammates and opponents to honor him. Gehrig, stricken by an incurable disease, gave his famous "luckiest man" speech that day.

The tradition officially started in 1946 when the Yankees invited their own alumni as well as old-timers from opposing clubs. For the first official Old-Timers' Day, the Yankees brought in 58-year-old Walter Johnson, the legendary Big Train, to pitch to Babe Ruth, who was 51. Ruth, diagnosed with throat cancer three months later, could only manage to hit a foul ball off Johnson but, to the fans' delight, broke into his famous home run trot nonetheless.

Nowadays, the event is an all-Yankee affair and one of the most popular events on the schedule. One reason is because of the newer "old-timers" who appear. Fans love seeing—and saluting—recently retired favorites such as Paul O'Neill and Tino Martinez. In 2007, five of the "old-timers" were younger than Roger Clemens, who started the regular game that day.

Other Old-Timers' Days have proved rather newsworthy. In a highly unpopular move, the Yankees released longtime shortstop Phil Rizzuto during the 1956 Old-Timers' Day ceremonies.

During the 1978 celebration, the Yankees stunned the crowd by announcing that Billy Martin, who had been fired five days earlier, would be "managing the Yankees in the 1980 season."

Another emotional Old-Timers' Day occurred in 1998. Former pitcher Jim Bouton, who became persona non grata with the Yankees for writing his controversial book *Ball Four* nearly 30 years earlier, returned from exile to wear pinstripes once again. Bouton's return was made possible by his son's article in *The New York Times*, asking the Yankees to forgive his dad. "Wearing that Yankee uniform again brought all those happy memories back when I was a kid in his 20s pitching for the best team in baseball history," Bouton said after his appearance. "I felt like I've finally been admitted back into the family."

2006 Old-Timers' Day: (from left) *Yogi Berra, Bob Turley, Charlie Silvera, Tommy Byrne, Don Larsen*

FIVE-O'CLOCK LIGHTNING

The Ruth-Gehrig teams of the 1920s were called "Murderers' Row," and those teams did a good part of their damage in the late innings. It often began with a mild, unassuming fellow named Earle Combs, a former Tennessee schoolteacher. Combs was a brilliant center fielder and a fleet-footed leadoff man, perhaps the greatest in Yankee history. He was known as the "Waiter," because he often waited to be driven around the bases by his teammates' explosive bats. Many times he waited on third base, due to his knack for hitting triples. He once hit three in a single game.

Back then, games started at 3:00 P.M., but the Yankees' didn't usually get their wakeup call until late afternoon. "The team struck so often in the late innings that Combs called this delayed attack 'five-o'clock lightning,'" wrote Frank Graham in his 1943 book, *The New York Yankees: An Informal History*. "The phrase caught on, spread through the league and seeped into the consciousness of opposing pitchers. They began to dread the approach of five o'clock and the eighth inning."

Earle Combs

The *Yankees*
don't pay me to win every day— just two out of three.

—CASEY STENGEL

FROM JOLTIN' JOE TO JAVA JOE

Beginning with his stellar 1936 rookie year, Joe DiMaggio became entrenched in pop culture.

1941: Record 56-game hitting streak inspires the hit song "Joltin' Joe DiMaggio," performed by the Les Brown Orchestra

1949: Broadway musical *South Pacific* includes a character named Bloody Mary with "skin as tender as DiMaggio's glove"

1952: Idolized by the old fisherman in Ernest Hemingway's classic novel *The Old Man and the Sea*

1954: Marries Hollywood icon Marilyn Monroe

1955: Elected to Baseball Hall of Fame

1968: Immortalized in Simon and Garfunkel's song "Mrs. Robinson," which is featured in the movie *The Graduate*

1969: Voted "Greatest Living Player" by fans as part of baseball's centennial celebration

1972: Makes first commercial for the Bowery Savings Bank

1974: Becomes TV pitchman for Mr. Coffee

1999: New York City's West Side Highway is renamed Joe DiMaggio Highway after his death at age 84

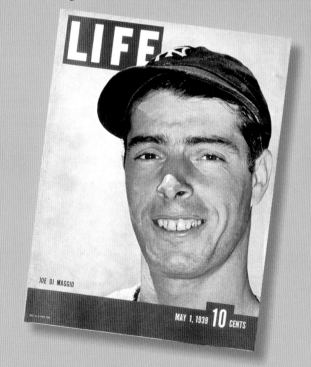

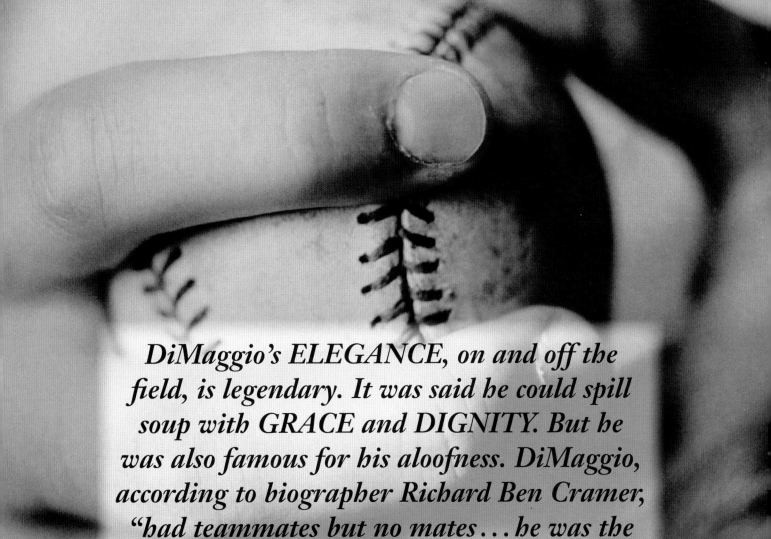

DiMaggio's ELEGANCE, on and off the field, is legendary. It was said he could spill soup with GRACE and DIGNITY. But he was also famous for his aloofness. DiMaggio, according to biographer Richard Ben Cramer, "had teammates but no mates...he was the LONELIEST hero we have ever had."

THE SULTAN OF NICKNAMES

George Herman Ruth will be forever known as "Babe," which he was first called in 1914 as a baby-faced 19-year-old with the minor-league Baltimore Orioles. Yet it seemed everyone—writers, fans, teammates, opponents—had a different name for him. Here are 26 other Ruth nicknames:

The Barnstorming Babe

The Battering Bambino

The Behemoth of Bust

The Big Bam	The King of Clout
The Bulky Monarch	King of Swing
The Caliph of Clout	The Maharajah of Mash
The Circuit Smasher	The Mammoth of Maul
The Goliath of Grand Slam	The (Big) Monk
The Great Bambino	The Raja of Rap
Herman the Great	The Slambino
His Eminence	The Sultan of Swat
Homeric Herman	The Wally of Wallop
The Home Run King	The Wazir of Wham
The Infant Swategy	The Wizard of Whack
Jidge	

THE McCARTHY ERA

DiMaggio and McCarthy

In the early 1930s, even baseball felt the impact of the Great Depression. Hard times made the game tougher and more desperate. Crowds dwindled, player salaries were cut, and austerity prevailed.

When the Yankees hired grim, no-nonsense manager Joe McCarthy in 1931, who would have guessed that happy days would soon return? After all, McCarthy was derided as a "busher" for kicking around in the minors for years and had just been fired as manager of the Cubs.

McCarthy brought law and order to the Yankees, who were coming off a third-place finish in 1930. He mercilessly drilled the team in fundamentals and demanded that players act and dress like big-leaguers. Beer drinking and card-playing were banned in the clubhouse. As pitcher Ed Wells said, "frivolity and fun" came to an end.

Confrontation with Babe Ruth—who still reveled in the good life of being a star—was inevitable, and within a few years, Ruth was released. Still, McCarthy held on, guiding the Yankees to a then-unmatched run of four consecutive world championships between 1936 and 1939.

Even then, Marse Joe was criticized as a "push-button manager" because he had been handed some great players including Lou Gehrig, Tony Lazzeri, Earle Combs, and Bill Dickey. But as Joe DiMaggio once said, "Never a day went by when you didn't learn something from McCarthy."

The fact remains that the Yankees won eight pennants and seven world championships during McCarthy's 16 seasons of pushing buttons in the Bronx.

PRIDE: THE MOVIE

Six months after Lou Gehrig's death, Hollywood producer Samuel Goldwyn bought the rights to Paul Gallico's best-selling biography *The Pride of the Yankees* to make it into a movie. Gary Cooper played the ill-fated Yankee star in the famed 1942 film, which is really more a love story than a baseball movie.

THE PRIVATE LIFE OF A PUBLIC HERO!

SAMUEL GOLDWYN presents **GARY COOPER**
THE PRIDE OF THE YANKEES
TERESA WRIGHT · WALTER BRENNAN and BABE RUTH Himself

YANKEES ABC'S

A A-Rod

He's probably the best and surely the richest player in baseball. In 2007, Alexander Emmanuel Rodriguez became the youngest player in history to reach 500 home runs. Yet ever since he came to the Yankees in 2004, A-Rod's been a lightning rod for controversy.

B Bleacher Creatures

That's the name for the relentlessly raucous collection of fans tucked behind Yankee Stadium's right field fence. From backless benches in Section 39, these uninhibited inhabitants started the first interactive chant in sports, the first-inning roll call, which prompts each Yankee starter to acknowledge the Creatures with a wave.

C Casey Stengel

The improvising, entertaining Ol' Perfessor was a well-traveled failure when he came to the Yankees in 1949 at age 58. Yet, the man with the clown reputation was also an astute student of the game. Charles Dillon Stengel won 10 pennants in 12 years with the Yankees, which is nothing to laugh at.

The 1927 Yankees were part of the first great Yankee dynasty.

D Dynasty

Chinese history is usually measured in relation to dynasties and so is Yankee history. No team has ruled its sport like the Yankees, from the glory of Ruth and Gehrig in the 1920s and '30s, to the grace of DiMaggio in the '40s, to the Mickey-Whitey-Yogi teams of the '50s and '60s, the Billy-Reggie-Munson "Bronx Zoo" of the '70s, and Torre's teams in the late '90s.

E Elston Howard

A man of uncommon class and quiet courage, Elston Gene Howard is a significant figure in Yankee history as its first African American player. He joined the team in 1955—eight years after Jackie Robinson had broken baseball's color barrier—and became one of the Yankees' most exceptional performers, helping them win pennants in nine of his first ten years.

TRADITION, TRADITION

No team cherishes tradition more than the Yankees. Yet the Yankees have a few—dare we say—quirky traditions. Take the "roll call," for example. In the first inning of each home game, the rowdies in the right field bleachers (also known as the Bleacher Creatures) chant the name of each position player, who then acknowledges the Creatures by waving his glove.

In the fifth inning, the grounds crew rake the infield and work up the crowd to the Village People's disco hit "YMCA." Several years ago, they changed to the song to "Macarena," but after the Yankees lost a few games an angry George Steinbrenner ordered the return of "YMCA." The music doesn't stop there. After each home victory, fans exit to Frank Sinatra's rendition of "New York, New York." If they lose, it's the Liza Minnelli version.

> 66 *I hit the jackpot. I came here at the right time. I played with the right people. Nobody could ask for that. You expect to win, but not the way we've won here.* 99
>
> —PAUL O'NEILL

THE GETTYSBURG ADDRESS OF BASEBALL

Lou Gehrig, feeling the effects of a progressive muscle disease that would take his life, gave his famous farewell speech to 61,808 fans at Yankee Stadium attending a "Lou Gehrig Day" doubleheader against the Washington Senators on July 4, 1939.

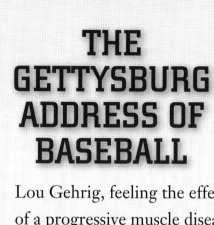

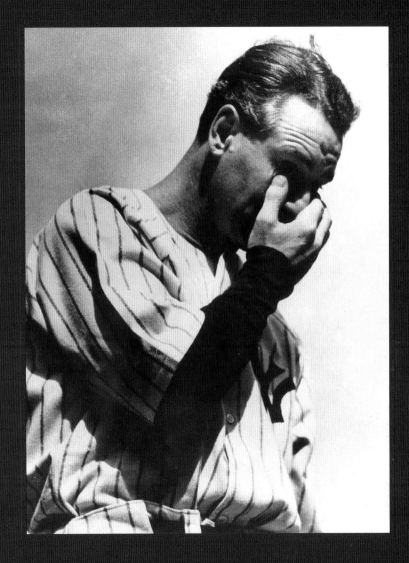

"Today I consider myself the luckiest man on the face of the earth."

—Lou Gehrig

MONUMENT PARK

The original Yankee Stadium featured three memorials in the deepest part of center field. That area was better known as Death Valley, but not because the memorials resembled headstones. (As a child, Billy Crystal was convinced Babe Ruth was buried there.) It got its name because, at 490 feet from home plate, it was where home runs went to die.

In 1932, the first stone monument was placed in front of the center field flagpole for Miller Huggins, Yankee manager from 1918 until his untimely death during the 1929 season. In 1941, another monument was dedicated to Lou Gehrig, about a month after his tragic death at age 37. Completing the monument troika was No. 3 himself, Babe Ruth. The Babe's monument was added on April 19, 1949, about seven months after his death.

The three stone memorials were in the field of play, leading to the occasional outfield adventure. So, when the stadium was remodeled in 1976, the Yankees created Monument Park behind the left field fence as a space to honor even more Yankee legends. There are now 5 monuments and 24 plaques.

When I was a little boy, I wanted to be a BASEBALL PLAYER and join a CIRCUS. With the Yankees, I've accomplished both.

—GRAIG NETTLES

CHAPTER TWO

BRONX TALES

"I get a thrill every time I put on my
Yankee uniform.
It sounds corny, but it's the gospel truth."

—Tommy Henrich

THE GOLDEN AGE

The years spanning 1947 to 1957—known in New York as the Golden Age—were some of the most eventful in baseball history. What made these years so golden? For starters, World War II was over and baseball players returned from the battlefield to the playing field. New stars and dramatic events seemed to proliferate. Eager for entertainment, many Americans turned their pent-up energy toward the national pastime.

The game also became a reflector of society's larger issues. In 1947, Jackie Robinson joined the Brooklyn Dodgers and integrated the sport. He became a representation of hope, justice, and opportunity. At the same time, television was entering the picture. The tube would profoundly affect the way Americans looked at sporting events and the way professional teams were financed.

But the Golden Age wasn't all about business. Baseball was still a game, and New York City was the center of the universe for many baseball fans. The Yankees and their National League rivals, the Giants and Dodgers, drew the fanatical attention of millions. In fact, in 1946, the first post-war season, the Yankees became the first team to draw more than two million fans.

Debates raged about the merits of New York's trio of famed centerfielders: Willie, Mickey, and the Duke. And who was better, Reese or Rizzuto? Campy or Yogi? One thing was certain: Never before and never again would a group of players dominate the game and the spirit of the city as New York's three teams did during the Golden Age. Baseball in New York, with its raging rivalries and long history of heroes and bums, attracted everyone's attention. The deeds and personalities of the Yankees, Giants, and Dodgers transformed a city of millions into a close-knit community of baseball fans. As writer Roger Angell said, baseball "was almost a private possession of New York City" during the 1950s.

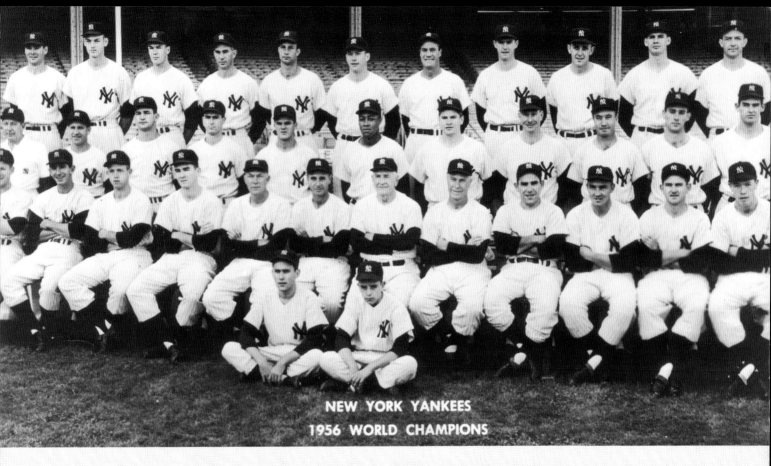

**NEW YORK YANKEES
1956 WORLD CHAMPIONS**

How dominant were the three teams? Except for the 1948 season, a New York City team competed in every World Series from 1947 to 1957. The Brooklyn Dodgers won six pennants and one world championship, the New York Giants won two pennants and one World Series, and the New York Yankees won an incredible nine pennants and seven world championships—five of them consecutive.

The Golden Age was a simpler time in New York City and the world, and the Yankees were simply the best.

Yankee Firsts

FIRST team to permanently wear numbers on the back of their uniforms (1929)

FIRST annual Old-Timers' Day event (1946)

FIRST team to hit a pinch homer in a World Series game (Yogi Berra, 1947)

FIRST team to use instant replay at the local level (1959)

FIRST team to have a player make a curtain call after a dramatic homer (Roger Maris, 1961) • • • • • •

FIRST team to employ an official designated hitter (Ron Blomberg, 1973)

Best Yankee Centerfielders

JOE DiMAGGIO (1936–1951)

MICKEY MANTLE (1951–1968)

BERNIE WILLIAMS (1991–2006)

EARLE COMBS (1924–1935)

MICKEY RIVERS (1976–1979)

YANKEE KILLERS

Here are some players who've made life miserable for the Bronx Bombers:

FRANK LARY: This Detroit pitcher won 27 career games against the Yankees.

EDGAR MARTINEZ: This Mariners DH annihilated the Yankees in the
1995 American League Division Series with a .571 average.

DAVID ORTIZ: Big Papi has been a chief Yankee tormenter since joining the Red Sox
in 2003.

JOHNNY PODRES: The Dodgers' 1955 World Series hero; his biography is entitled
Brooklyn's Yankee Killer.

HOYT WILHELM: This knuckleballer pitched a no-hitter against the Yankees in
1958, the only no-hitter against the team in 45 years.

On May 28, 1946, the Yankees played their first night game at Yankee Stadium, drawing 49,917 fans. The Yankees lost, 2–1, to the Washington Senators.

YANKEE NICKNAMES

- Lawrence **"YOGI"** Berra: He grew up in St. Louis, where as a kid his friends saw him cross his legs and fold his arms while watching a game. They said he looked like a yogi.

- Joe **"YANKEE CLIPPER"** or **"JOLT-IN' JOE"** DiMaggio: Broadcaster Arch McDonald noted that the great outfielder's grace and swiftness was reminiscent of a Yankee Clipper sailing ship. "Joltin' Joe DiMaggio" was the title of a popular 1941 ditty.

- Whitey **"CHAIRMAN OF THE BOARD"** Ford: This crafty Hall of Fame lefty was given his moniker by catcher Elston Howard for his cool confidence and efficiency.

- Lou **"THE IRON HORSE"** Gehrig: This powerful and durable star was nick-named after the powerful and durable locomotives of the Old West.

- Vernon **"LEFTY"** or **"GOOFY"** Gomez: A zany left-handed pitching star of the 1930s, he kept teammates loose with his wit. He was called "Goofy" for claiming he had invented a revolving fishbowl for tired goldfish.

- Ron **"GATOR"** or **"LOUISIANA LIGHTNING"** Guidry: A native of Louisiana and an ardent fisherman and hunter, Guidry was dubbed "Gator" because of his background. Announcer Phil Rizzuto began calling him "Louisiana Lightning."

- Tommy **"OLD RELIABLE"** Henrich: This clutch hitter and fielder was given his nickname by announcer Mel Allen.

- Jim **"CATFISH"** Hunter: This North Carolina farm boy was called "Catfish" as a publicity gimmick by Kansas City A's owner Charlie Finley, who signed him in 1964.

- Reggie **"MR. OCTOBER"** Jackson: His heroics in the playoffs and World Series prompted this appropriate nickname.

- Tony **"POOSH 'EM UP"** Lazzeri: He was an early baseball hero of Italian-Americans, who yelled "Poosh 'em up, Tony!" during the late 1920s and '30s, as Lazzeri frequently advanced runners with his timely hitting.

- Hideki **"GODZILLA"** Matsui: This Japanese outfielder got his moniker from high school classmates for his acne problem, but it later reflected his monster home runs as the Japanese League's biggest star.

- Don **"DONNIE BASEBALL"** Mattingly: This popular first baseman was given his nickname by opponent Kirby Puckett for his remarkable dedication and drive.

- Graig **"PUFF"** Nettles: This wisecracking third baseman would interject a joke in conversations with his teammates—then disappear like a puff of smoke.

- Vic **"THE SPRINGFIELD RIFLE"** Raschi: He was nicknamed in honor of his hometown, Springfield, Massachusetts, and his trademark pitch, a blazing eye-high fastball.

- Phil **"SCOOTER"** Rizzuto: This shortstop was nicknamed for the way he ran after groundballs as a young player.

- Casey **"THE OL' PERFESSOR"** Stengel: His nickname came from his time at the University of Mississippi in 1914, where he helped coach the baseball team and was appointed a professor.

Teresa Brewer was a 25-year-old pop singer when she introduced

a novelty tune created during 24-year-old slugger Mickey Mantle's 1956 Triple Crown season.

Bobby Murcer

Mickey Mantle

IDOL CHATTER

How do you fill the shoes of a legend? Young Bobby Murcer was touted, perhaps unfairly, as the next Mickey Mantle when he became the Yankees' center fielder in 1969. Murcer was no Mantle, but who was? Instead, Murcer was the best player on the mediocre Yankee teams of the early '70s. Over his 17-year career, he batted .277 with 252 home runs, once hitting home runs in four consecutive at bats. Always a gentleman, he was a Yankee broadcaster for more than 20 years and became one of the team's most beloved figures.

OUTSIDE THE HALL

ROGER MARIS'S YANKEE STATS 1960–1966

Games	Hits	HR	RBI	Avg.
850	797	203	547	.265

<u>NOTABLE ACHIEVEMENTS:</u>

- American League MVP, 1960 and 1961
- Broke Babe Ruth's single-season home run record of 60 (set in 1927), hitting 61 in 1961
- Played on five pennant-winning Yankee teams and two world championship teams

"He should waltz right into the Hall of Fame. Why he's not in, it should be an embarrassment to baseball."

—YANKEE PITCHER RALPH TERRY ON FORMER TEAMMATE ROGER MARIS IN *BASEBALL DIGEST, 2005*

Yankees' All Non-Hall of Fame Team

Catcher: Thurman Munson (1969–1979)

First base: Don Mattingly (1982–1995)

Second base: Willie Randolph (1976–1988)

Shortstop: Tony Kubek (1957–1965)

Third base: Graig Nettles (1973–1983)

Left field: Bob Meusel (1920–1929)

Center field: Bernie Williams (1991–2006)

Right field: Roger Maris (1960–1966)

Right-handed starter: Spud Chandler (1937–1947)

Left-handed starter: Ron Guidry (1975–1988)

Reliever: Johnny Murphy (1932–1943, 1946)

Manager: Billy Martin (1975–1979, 1983, 1985, 1988)

Note: Years with Yankees listed. List excludes current Yankees.

PASSING THE TORCH

By the 1950s, Joe DiMaggio was winding down. At age 36 and battling injuries, he was simply not able to play as he once had. How would the Yankees make up for his grandeur and spectacular talent?

In 1951, the Yankees would get a glimpse of DiMaggio's replacement. His name was Mickey Charles Mantle. This raw gem from the zinc mines of Oklahoma reported to the Yankees' Phoenix training camp that season with little public notice. He was a 19-year-old, wild-armed shortstop from the Class C Joplin, Missouri, farm team. Nobody expected him to make the big club that year. Then again, nobody expected him to hit .402 or smash Herculean home runs that spring either. By Opening Day, he was in right field in Yankee Stadium, playing alongside the great DiMaggio, in front of more fans than he'd ever seen. It's safe to say no rookie had ever started a season with such incredible fanfare since DiMaggio had back in 1936. As manager Casey Stengel put it, "The kid is jumping five classifications at once and is going into a strange position. If he can make it, he's a wonder."

Many debated whether or not Mantle could cut it, and all the hype seemed to hurt him. He tensed up and started to pout, and when he slumped the fans booed him mercilessly. By mid-July, he was sent to the Kansas City farm club. Mantle told his dad he didn't think he was up to playing in the big leagues. But his father—who was determined that his son should be a professional ballplayer—challenged him. Mickey responded. He learned to play center in Kansas City, so he could eventually succeed DiMaggio.

Later that season, he was recalled by the Yankees and again was in right field when the World Series began. In Game 2, he and DiMaggio chased after a Willie Mays fly ball. Suddenly, Mantle tripped on a drain and fell hard. DiMaggio made the catch and hastened to where the rookie lay motionless, waving for a stretcher.

It would be the first of many serious knee injuries of Mantle's career. Like DiMaggio, he would go on to play through disabling pain, earn enormous respect from his teammates, and become the Yankees' signature player and the idol of millions. Throughout the 1950s and '60s, he played the glamour position on baseball's glamour team. In his first 14 seasons as a Yankee, he played in 12 World Series. The torch had been passed.

Mantle and DiMaggio

	Games	AB	R	H	HR	RBI	SO	SB	AVG
DiMaggio (1936–1951)	1,736	6,821	1,390	2,214	361	1,537	369	30	.325
Mantle (1951–1968)	2,401	8,102	1,677	2,415	536	1,509	1,710	153	.298

*Brian Doyle goes toe-to-toe with the Dodgers'
Johnny Oates in the 1978 World Series.*

FALL GUYS: UNLIKELY WORLD SERIES HEROES

1953 BILLY MARTIN

This lifetime .257 hitter went 12-for-24 against Brooklyn to help give the Yankees their fifth-straight championship. In the previous year, also against the Dodgers, he made a lunging, Series-saving catch in Game 7.

1956 DON LARSEN

This journeyman right-hander, who only two years earlier was 3–21 with the Baltimore Orioles, pitched the only perfect game in World Series history against a powerful Brooklyn lineup and captured MVP honors.

1960 BOBBY RICHARDSON

After hitting only .252 with 26 RBI in the regular season, this second baseman led the Yankees by hitting .367 with 12 RBI against Pittsburgh. However, the Yankees still lost on Bill Mazeroski's dramatic home run.

1978 BRIAN DOYLE

He was called up during the regular season to replace the injured Willie Randolph at second base, and he batted .192 in 39 games. In the Series, though, he destroyed the Dodgers with a .438 average in six games.

1996 JIM LEYRITZ

A mediocre hitter and part-time player, Leyritz—who entered Game 4 in the sixth inning to replace catcher Joe Girardi—hit a three-run, Series-changing home run in the eighth inning against the Braves.

2000 LUIS SOJO

A well-traveled role player who appeared in only 34 games for the Yankees in the regular season, Sojo delivered a dramatic two-out, two-run single in the ninth inning against the Mets' Al Leiter to win the Series. It was the Yankees' third consecutive world championship.

BRING ON THE PLATOON

Casey Stengel wasn't the first manager to use the platoon system in baseball—his mentor John McGraw had actually platooned Stengel as a player with the New York Giants in the 1920s. But Stengel was the first to platoon on a large scale when he took over as Yankee manager in 1949.

Actually, he was forced to when the team was decimated by injuries. Red Patterson, the Yankees public relations director, listed 72 major and minor injuries to the team, which included Joe DiMaggio being out until June with a heel spur.

The Yankees used seven first basemen that season, including outfielder Tommy Henrich for 52 games. When Henrich caught the last out against Boston to end the season and give the Yankees the pennant, coach Bill Dickey jumped up in the dugout and cracked his head on the roof. "That made 73," said trainer Gus Mauch.

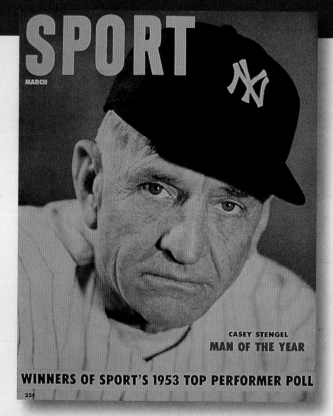

SPORT

MARCH

CASEY STENGEL
MAN OF THE YEAR

WINNERS OF SPORT'S 1953 TOP PERFORMER POLL

25¢

Stengel preached versatility, and nobody typified that better than Gil McDougald, who became an All-Star at three different positions— second base, shortstop, and third base. By the mid-1950s, platooning was commonplace in baseball.

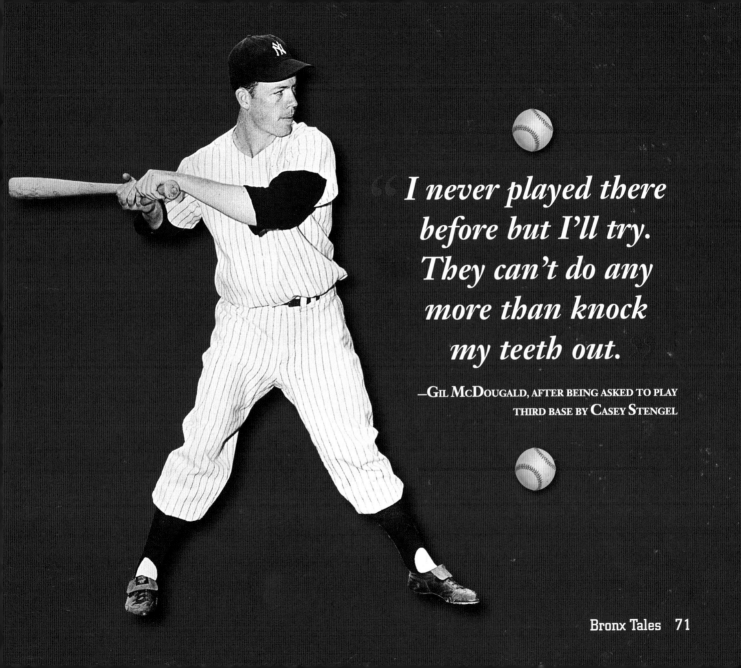

> *I never played there before but I'll try. They can't do any more than knock my teeth out.*

—GIL MCDOUGALD, AFTER BEING ASKED TO PLAY THIRD BASE BY CASEY STENGEL

YANKEES ABC'S

F Frieze

The decorative copper facing along the roof of old Yankee Stadium was the signature feature of the House That Ruth Built. It gave the place an aura of dignity, which was sadly lost when the frieze was removed during the 1970s renovation. Now, the frieze is back as a prominent feature in the new Yankee Stadium.

G George Herman Ruth

The greatest player ever is a man called Babe. He helped save the game in the wake of the Black Sox scandal in 1919, electrified audiences with his home run prowess, and continued to amaze Americans with his incredible combination of charisma, power, and style.

Ruth with two young fans

H Holy Cow!

This is the trademark phrase of lovable broadcaster Phil Rizzuto, who entertained Yankee fans with his loopy banter and childlike enthusiasm for more than 40 years. Most viewers and listeners never saw the Hall of Fame shortstop play for the Yankees in the 1940s and '50s, but Scooter attracted generations of new fans with his offbeat style in the booth.

I Interlocking "NY"

The Yankee NY is the most recognizable sports logo on the planet. Louis Comfort Tiffany created the interlocking NY logo in 1877. It became a permanent part of the Yankee uniform in 1936 but has appeared on Yankee caps since 1909.

Phil Rizzuto (left) *with fellow broadcaster Pee Wee Reese*

THE FIRST BLACK YANKEE

One shameful element of Yankee history is that General Manager George Weiss for years excluded African Americans from the team. Not exactly a social activist, Weiss cynically felt his team didn't need black players because it was winning without them.

That finally changed on April 14, 1955—one day short of eight years after Jackie Robinson broke baseball's color barrier—when a soft-spoken, 26-year-old catcher-outfielder named Elston Howard took the field for the Yankees at Fenway Park.

Howard, a former star in the Negro Leagues, got in the lineup after teammate Irv Noren was ejected over a call. In integrating the Yankees—the 13th of 16 teams to field a black player—Howard proved to be a perfect fit. From

the start, the reception from his teammates was always warm. As long as he could do the job, they didn't care what color he was. And Howard could do the job.

He was a dignified man and a versatile player, working the outfield and first base, and catching (when Yogi Berra needed a break). Ultimately he replaced Yogi and played the position with the best of them, becoming a master handler of pitchers while posting a .993 career fielding average.

"It took me a while, I think, before I developed fully as a player and was appreciated fully for my ability," Howard told author Peter Golenbock in *Dynasty*. "By 1963, of course, I had taken over full-time for Yogi and I won the MVP. That's the Nobel Prize of baseball."

Mickey Mantle, Elston Howard, and Hank Bauer

<blockquote>
"A man of great gentleness
and DIGNITY."
</blockquote>

—FROM ELSTON HOWARD'S PLAQUE IN MONUMENT PARK

FARM FRESH

Yankee stars came and went from the 1930s
through the early '60s, but the team never missed
a beat. There were always talented reinforce-
ments down on the farm. The Yankees' far-flung
farm system was once the envy of baseball.
Branch Rickey pioneered the concept with the
Cardinals, but farm director George Weiss per-
fected it with the Yankees. At one point the Yankees had more than 20 minor-league teams, and
Weiss supervised every detail of their operation.

Jacob Ruppert brought in Weiss in 1932 to
create a replenishing feeder system, and the tire-
less Weiss quickly went to work. By 1937, the
Newark Bears of the International League became so powerful that many believed they were
superior to several major-league clubs. Because
of their minor-league talent surplus, the Yankees
could always swap a young prospect for an established veteran to help during a pennant race.

Free agency was still in the future, so the
Yankees developed the best players by putting
huge emphasis on scouting, instruction, funda-

Charlie Keller was a product of the Yankee farm system.

mentals, and teaching the Yankee way. Ultimately, the Yankee farm system was a starting point
for many future major-league stars, including
Charlie Keller, Phil Rizzuto, Yogi Berra, Mickey
Mantle, and Gil McDougald.

We're Number 1

The Yankees retired No. 1 in honor of Billy Martin, but he wasn't the first to wear it. These players also wore the number:

Earle Combs (1929–1935)

Roy Johnson (1936)

Frank Crosetti (1937–1943)

Tuck Stainback (1944)

Snuffy Stirnweiss (1945–1950)

Bobby Richardson (1958–1966)

Bobby Murcer (1969–1974)

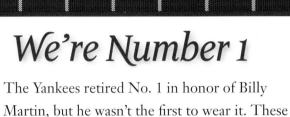

Bobby Richardson

THE BIG THREE

From 1949 to 1953, not one Yankee hitter led the league in any offensive category. No matter. They still managed to rewrite baseball history, winning five consecutive championships. Suffice it to say that it wouldn't have happened without the Big Three—the oft-overlooked pitching greats Vic Raschi, Allie Reynolds, and Ed Lopat. None of them are in the Hall of Fame or have a plaque in Monument Park. Still, they're remembered for their many wins and fierce competitiveness.

Raschi, a bulldog on the mound, won 21 games in three consecutive seasons (1949–1951). Reynolds, a Native American who threw as hard as anyone in the game, was at his best when the stakes were high. He was particularly effective in the World Series when he'd come in from the bullpen to close games. Lopat, a lefty control pitcher who threw an assortment of "junk," was a perfect complement to the fireball offerings of Raschi and Reynolds.

Allie Reynolds

The trio won 255 games, losing 117, for the Yankees from 1949 to 1953, exclusive of their World Series triumphs. Years later, when the legendary Branch Rickey was asked to name the greatest pitching staff he ever saw, he said, "Raschi, Reynolds, and Lopat."

When asked how he could say that considering all the great pitchers he'd seen in 60 years in baseball, he said, "Well, to make it short and sweet, you name me another staff that won five straight pennants and five straight World Series. When it got toughest, they always won."

From left to right: Lopat, Stengel, Raschi, and Reynolds

“ *He was the **best pitcher** at starting and relieving I've ever managed. In fact, I'd go further and tell you he's the **best** at the two things that I've ever seen. What I mean is, he's two pitchers rolled into one.* ”

—Casey Stengel on Allie Reynolds

THE VOICE

A native of Alabama with a friendly, spirited style, Mel Allen greeted millions of fans each day with, "Hello there everybody," as the comforting "Voice of the Yankees" from 1939 to 1964. Yankee followers adored Allen, yet he was more than a local institution. *Variety* magazine said he had one of the 25 most recognizable voices in the world. Of course, broadcasting more World Series games than anyone in history helped to enhance his reputation.

Mel Allen was also a great raconteur and pitchman. He called home runs "Ballantine Blasts" and "White Owl Wallops" in deference to the team's sponsors. Allen also pioneered the home run call, "Going, going, gone!" And after a great play, he'd exclaim, "How about that!"

Allen also created popular player nicknames, such as Tommy "Old Reliable" Henrich, "Steady Eddie" Lopat, Hank "Man of the Hour" Bauer, and Allie "Superchief" Reynolds.

Fireworks and Duds: Yankee Fourth of July Events

1930 George Steinbrenner is born.

1939 On Lou Gehrig Day, the Iron Horse's uniform No. 4 is retired.

1954 Pitcher Jim Beattie is born.

1983 Dave Righetti pitches a no-hitter against the Red Sox at Yankee Stadium.

2006 Cleveland overpowers the Yankees 19–1 at Yankee Stadium.

STREAKS ALIVE!

DON MATTINGLY homered in eight consecutive games in 1987, tying Dale Long's major-league record set in 1956.

JOE DiMAGGIO hit in a record 56 consecutive games in 1941.

YOGI BERRA played in 148 consecutive games (from July 28, 1957, to May 10, 1959) behind the plate without an error.

LOU GEHRIG played in 2,130 consecutive games.

WHITEY FORD pitched 33⅔ combined scoreless innings in World Series play from 1960 to 1962, breaking the record Babe Ruth had set with the Red Sox.

THE YANKEES won an unprecedented five straight World Series (1949–1953).

THE YANKEES won 14 straight World Series games, beginning in the 1996 Series and ending in 2000.

PA announcer **BOB SHEPPARD** called 121 consecutive playoff games, his streak ending at age 97 in 2007 due to a bronchial infection.

Gehrig and DiMaggio

"The more we lose, the more **Steinbrenner** *will fly in. And the more he flies, the better the chance there will be for a plane crash."*

—Graig Nettles on the benefits of a losing streak

SUMMER OF '56

In his native home in the Ozarks, scout Tom Greenwade used to arrange hunting trips with Harry Truman in his pre-presidential days. Yet it's safe to say his greatest accomplishment was bagging a young buck from northeastern Oklahoma named Mickey Mantle, whom he signed to the Yankees in 1949. Green-wade told his bosses the kid had a chance to be "a great ballplayer."

"Great" doesn't begin to describe Mantle's signature season with the Yankees, which cemented his status as a superstar. As Mantle wrote in his book, *My Favorite Summer, 1956*, "Everything just seemed to go right for me that year. The big thing was I was healthy and it seemed every-thing else just kind of fell into place."

In 1956, Mantle became the first Triple Crown winner since 1947. He hit amazingly long home runs and almost hit a fair ball out of Yankee Stadium for the first time in history. In the May 30 game against Washington, he banged a ball off the frieze, just 18 inches shy of clearing the roof. He batted .353, smashed 52 home runs, and drove in 130 runs. In the summer of '56, he became the greatest box-office draw in the game.

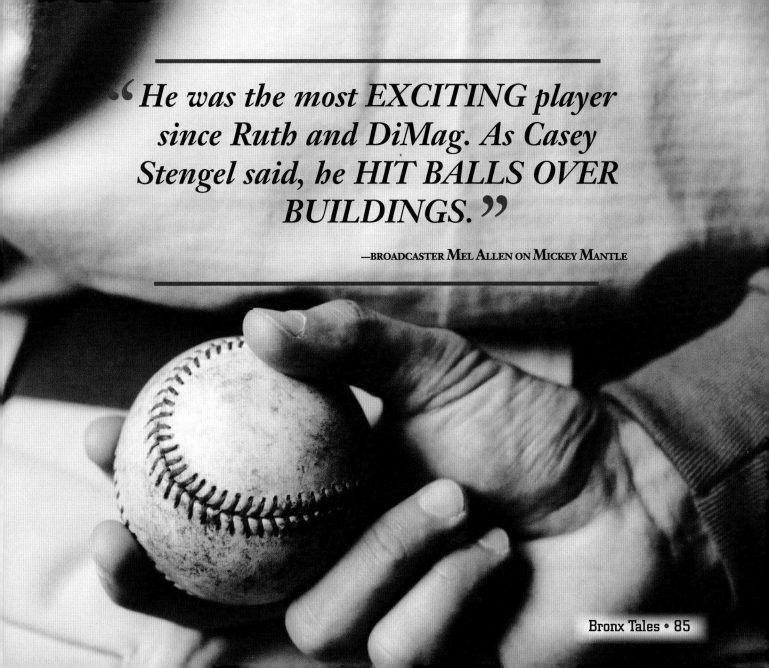

> "He was the most EXCITING player since Ruth and DiMag. As Casey Stengel said, he HIT BALLS OVER BUILDINGS."
>
> —BROADCASTER MEL ALLEN ON MICKEY MANTLE

REPLACING THE STARS

BABE RUTH (OF)

George Selkirk wore Ruth's No. 3 and took the right field job in 1935, hitting over .300 in four consecutive seasons.

MICKEY MANTLE (OF)

When Mickey became a first baseman in 1967, flaky first baseman Joe Pepitone switched to center for two seasons, before Mantle protégé Bobby Murcer took over.

PAUL O'NEILL (OF)

When popular "Paulie" retired in 2001, right field became a black hole. Shane Spencer led the parade of 2002 disappointments, which also included John Vander Wal, Juan Rivera, and Raul Mondesi.

LOU GEHRIG (1B)

Babe Dahlgren took over for the ailing Gehrig on May 2, 1939, hitting a homer in his first game. He remained the Yankee first baseman for only two seasons.

WILLIE RANDOLPH (2B)

Steve Sax took over in 1989 for the reliable Randolph. Sax made two All-Star trips in three seasons in the Bronx.

PHIL RIZZUTO (SS)

After Scooter was unceremoniously released during the 1956 season, jack-of-all-trades Gil McDougald took over for 1½ seasons.

GRAIG NETTLES (3B)

The Yankees originally brought in Toby Harrah to platoon with Nettles, but then they traded Nettles to San Diego during spring training in 1984. Harrah flopped sharing third with Mike Pagliarulo and was gone the next season.

THURMAN MUNSON (C)

Rick Cerone was acquired from Toronto three months after Munson's tragic 1979 plane crash. Cerone responded to the unenviable challenge of replacing the beloved captain with the best season of his 18-year career.

Graig Nettles

Bronx Tales • 87

DID YOU KNOW?

- A federal court in 1937 awarded $7,500 to David Levy, whose skull had been fractured in a scuffle with Yankee Stadium ushers when he tried to retrieve a foul ball hit by Lou Gehrig in 1934. As a result, major-league clubs decided that fans could keep balls hit into the stands.

- The Yankees were the first team to draw more than one million fans in home attendance when they drew 1,289,422 fans at the Polo Grounds in 1920. They were also the first team to draw more than two million fans for a season, when they attracted 2,265,512 in 1946.

- In 2000, Derek Jeter became the first player to be named Most Valuable Player of both the All-Star Game and World Series in the same season.

- The longest game in Yankee history was on June 24, 1962, when the Yankees battled the Tigers in a seven-hour, 22-inning marathon in Detroit. The Yankees won 9–7 on a home run by Jack Reed, the only homer of his major-league career.

Derek Jeter

DR. YOGI

Besides being a legendary catcher, Yogi Berra is an accidental philosopher and perhaps the most quoted man in the country. Many people probably know him more for his "Yogi-isms" than his brilliance behind the plate from the late 1940s to the early '60s.

Here's what he told the graduating class at Montclair State University in 1996 when he received an honorary degree in humanities:

"I am happy to speak my words at the university graduation. A lot of people have been quoting me ever since I came to play for the Yankees in 1946. But, as I once said, I really didn't say everything I said. So now it's my turn. I want to give some of my famous advice to the graduates. First, never give up, because it ain't over 'til it's over. Second, during the years ahead, when you come to the fork in the road, take it. Third, don't always follow the crowd, because nobody goes there any more. It's too crowded. Fourth, stay alert. You can observe a lot by watching. Fifth, and last, remember that whatever you do in life, 90 percent of it is half mental. In closing, I want to quote myself again: Thank you, Montclair State University, for making this day necessary."

THE HORACE CLARKE ERA

Whitey Ford had little left. Mickey Mantle was limping to the end. The holdovers from the early 1960s championship teams were fading and retiring. They were being replaced by non-stalwarts. By the mid-1960s, the Yankees seemed like a masquerade version of themselves. The once-fertile farm system had dry-rotted. A glorious era was over. The years 1965 to 1975 were lean times in Yankee history and became known as the Horace Clarke Era.

So who exactly was Horace Clarke and why did he have an era named after him? Good question. Truth be told, Clarke was a decent ballplayer. He was a contact-hitting infielder who was the best major-leaguer ever to come from the Virgin Islands. When Bobby Richardson retired after the 1966 season—in which the Yankees finished in 10th place, the worst in their history—Clarke was given the job at second base.

A switch-hitting leadoff man, he was hardly a rabble-rouser. "Hoss" was a quiet fellow and a durable fixture for seven seasons (1966–1973), averaging 151 games per season. He stole bases and was a pesky hitter who actually broke up three no-hit bids in one month. More often than not, he's remembered for wearing a batting helmet while playing second base and for his inability to turn a double play with runners barreling in on him.

Clarke absorbed a lot of guff for this shortcoming. So did manager Ralph Houk, who later told author Bill Madden in *Pride of the Yankees:* "I know I got a lot of criticism for playing Horace Clarke as much as I did, but he was a lot better ballplayer than anyone gave him credit for. He did a lot of things good but nothing great, and that was his problem...besides, I didn't have anyone else."

TEN DEGREES OF
Yankees
SEPARATION

Melky Cabrera was the Yankees' Opening Day center fielder in 2008. He happened to be a teammate and successor of Bernie Williams,

who was a teammate of Don Mattingly,

who played with Bobby Murcer,

who played with Mickey Mantle,

who played with Joe DiMaggio,

who played with Lou Gehrig,

who played with Wally Pipp,

who played with Birdie Cree,

who played with Wee Willie Keeler,

who was the starting right fielder on April 22, 1903, the day the Yankees (then the Highlanders) played their first game.

Melky Cabrera

THE BRONX IS BURNING

When a raging fire broke out near Yankee Stadium during the 1977 World Series, broadcaster Howard Cosell intoned, "There it is, ladies and gentlemen, the Bronx is burning."

In actuality Cosell described more than a flash news story. It was a blighted, decadent time in New York City, with a new crisis always looming. A July blackout plunged the city into darkness, which erupted into a frenzy of looting and arson. The serial killer named Son of Sam preyed on young couples, striking fear everywhere. To top it off, the near-bankrupt city didn't have enough firefighters or police officers to deal with the mounting problems.

New York badly needed something to cheer about in the summer of '77. So the resurgent (and bickering) Yankees—who had not won a World Series in 15 years—became a riveting sideshow. The brash Reggie Jackson battled all season with his hot-tempered manager, Billy Martin, and led the Yankees to the championship in storybook fashion.

Eventually the saga of the city and the Yankees became a best-selling book by Jonathan Mahler and inspired an ESPN miniseries in 2007. Cosell's terse observation provided the catchy title, *The Bronx Is Burning*.

Martin and Jackson argue in the dugout.

CRYSTAL CLEAR FAN

There's Denzel, the Donald, Regis, and even Henry Kissinger—all celebrity Yankee fans. But they're not in the same ballpark when it comes to Billy Crystal's pinstriped passion. To honor his 60th birthday, the team let the actor-comedian suit up and get an at-bat during an exhibition game in March 2008.

Crystal called it the greatest thrill of his life. The second greatest was probably when his father took him to his first game at Yankee Stadium on May 30, 1956. He was eight years old, and his dad had arranged beforehand with trainer Gus Mauch to take his son to the clubhouse level.

"You can imagine how exciting that was for a little kid," Crystal told *The New York Times.* "Gus came out and talked to us and then took my program inside and brought it out with all the signatures on it. Casey Stengel came out in the hall and I remember saying, 'Who's pitching today, Casey?' and he looked at me and said, 'You are, kid, suit up.' How could you not be a Yankees fan after that?"

Like legions of youngsters in the 1950s, Crystal was smitten with Mickey Mantle. "It was Mickey that made you want to be a Yankees fan," he said. "He was so cool. He looked like a movie star. If you liked James Dean or Elvis, then you liked Mickey."

Later, as Crystal established himself in show business, he became friends with Mantle, although he admitted he always felt like he was eight years old with him. Several years after Mantle's death, Crystal paid $239,000 for his glove at an auction. And then he directed *61**, an HBO movie about the 1961 season that Mantle and Roger Maris slugged it out in a head-to-head home run race. "It was the greatest summer you could ever imagine," he said. "I loved them both, but Mickey was clearly my choice."

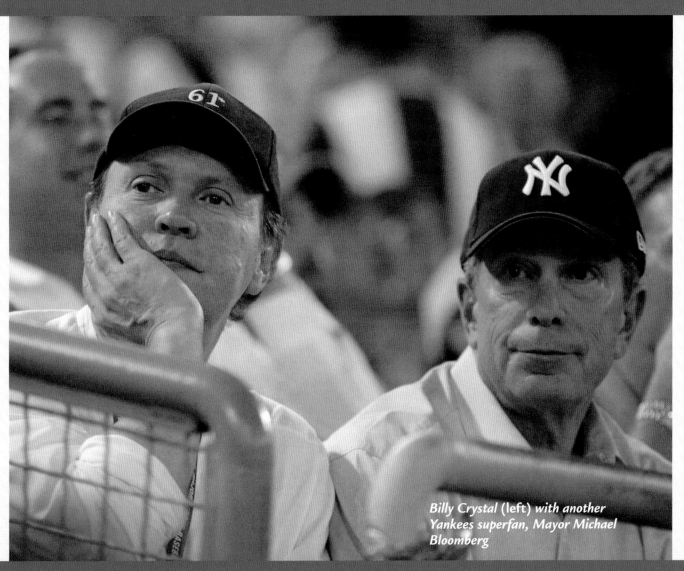

Billy Crystal (left) **with another Yankees superfan, Mayor Michael Bloomberg**

TOP YANKEE MOVIES

- *The Pride of the Yankees* (1942)
  This film is an inspiring portrayal of the ill-fated Lou Gehrig, played by Gary Cooper.

- *61** (2001)
  Billy Crystal meticulously portrays the dramatic home run race between Mickey Mantle and Roger Maris.

- *The Bronx Is Burning* (2007)
  An eight-part miniseries on ESPN about the tumultuous 1977 Yankees. John Turturro is excellent as the embattled Billy Martin.

- *Damn Yankees* (1958)
  A fun musical starring Gwen Verdon and Tab Hunter, who plays a Washington Senators fan who sells his soul to beat the Yankees. It's based on the novel *The Year the Yankees Lost the Pennant*.

BRONX BOMBS

- *The Babe Ruth Story* (1948)
  Arguably the worst baseball film ever, with William Bendix as a silly travesty of the title role.

- *The Babe* (1992)
  It's an obvious upgrade from the earlier Ruth film, with John Goodman giving an earnest effort. Still, it's just not Ruthian.

- *Safe at Home!* (1962)
  The implausibly hokey story about a kid who brags he knows Mickey Mantle and Roger Maris, who play themselves in the film.

- *The Scout* (1994)
  Albert Brooks plays a Yankee scout in this drab, fictionalized story.

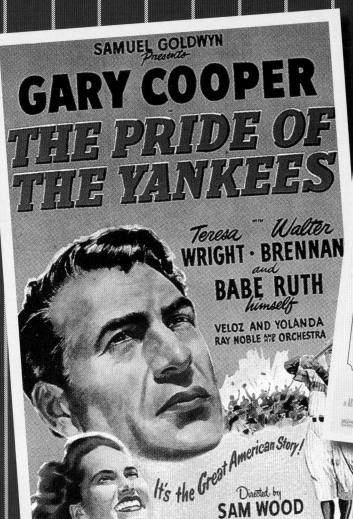

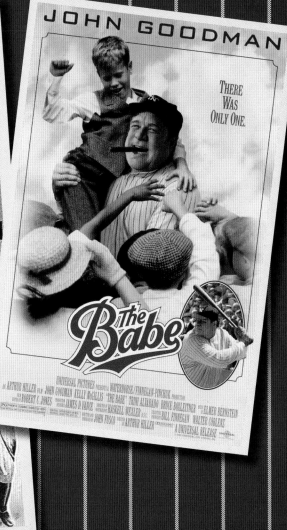

CHAPTER THREE

PRIDE IN PINSTRIPES

" God, I hope I wear this jersey forever. "

—Derek Jeter

M&M BOYS

In the summer of 1961, a pair of Yankee sluggers engaged in a magnificent assault on baseball's Holy Grail: Babe Ruth's 1927 single-season record of 60 home runs. Mickey Mantle and Roger Maris—the M&M Boys—put on quite a show.

Their dramatic duel occurred during a year of expansion. It was the league's first 10-team, 162-game season. It was also the first time in 12 years that the Yankees had a new manager (Ralph Houk). At the same time, the Yankees were involved in a heated pennant race with Detroit.

Still, the Mantle-Maris pursuit of Ruth's record overshadowed everything else. By the end of July, Mantle had 38 homers and Maris had 40. That's when commissioner Ford Frick—Ruth's close friend and ghostwriter—issued his "asterisk" decree. If either broke Ruth's record of 60 home runs, it would have to be achieved by game number 154 to be official, as Babe had only played that many games in his record season.

The last two months were a media circus. Leg injuries sidelined Mantle (who wound up with 54) and Maris began feeling pressure, anxiety, a loss of privacy—and a loss of hair. Maris, a small-town guy from North Dakota, was uncomfortable in the big-city spotlight. Most of the public hoped that the popular Mantle would break Ruth's record, instead of the shy, sullen Maris who was only in his second year with the Yankees.

On the final day of the season, Maris was tied with the Babe at 60. He came to bat at Yankee Stadium against Boston's Tracy Stallard and lined a shot into the right-field stands for number 61.

Only 23,154 fans—less than half of Yankee Stadium's capacity—were on hand to see Maris break the seemingly unbreakable record. His immortal feat notwithstanding—his home run record lasted for 37 years—Maris was something of a sad figure, often unappreciated and underrated. He was only 51 when he died.

Maris and Mantle

Did You Know?

- During his record-breaking season, Roger Maris drew no intentional walks. Many believe this happened because Mantle batted cleanup behind Maris, and he was the more feared slugger of the two.

- Maris smashed homers 37, 38, 39, and 40 on July 25, 1961, in a doubleheader against the White Sox.

- A 19-year-old fan from Coney Island named Sal Durante caught Maris's 61st home run ball. He received $5,000 and a trip to the Seattle World's Fair for the ball.

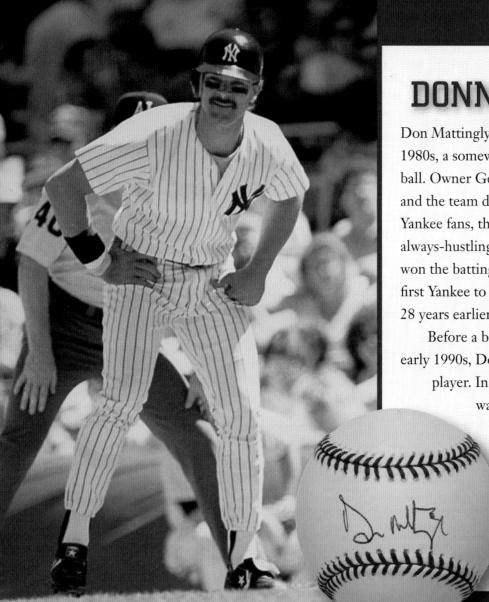

DONNIE BASEBALL

Don Mattingly was the homegrown hero of the 1980s, a somewhat wretched era of Yankee baseball. Owner George Steinbrenner behaved badly, and the team didn't perform much better. For Yankee fans, the only joy was to watch the always-hustling, torrid-hitting Mattingly. He won the batting title in his first full season, the first Yankee to do so since Mickey Mantle won it 28 years earlier.

Before a bad back doomed his career in the early 1990s, Don Mattingly was a remarkable player. In 1985, his second full season, he was league MVP. In 1986, he became the first player in 25 years to hit .350 with 30 home runs. From 1984 to 1989, he drove in 100 runs five times. Mattingly also collected a total of nine Gold Gloves.

Yankee Owners

OWNER (YEARS OWNED)	PENNANTS	CHAMPIONSHIPS
George M. Steinbrenner (1973–present)	10	6
CBS[1] (1964–1973)	0	0
Dan Topping, Del Webb, Larry MacPhail[2] (1945–1964)	15	10
Jacob Ruppert (1922–1945)	13	10
Jacob Ruppert, Tillinghast Huston[3] (1915–1922)	1	0
Frank Farrell, Bill Devery (1903–1915)	0	0

Rudy Giuliani, George Steinbrenner, and Joe Torre celebrate the Yankees' 1996 World Series victory.

[1] CBS bought the team in August 1964, one month before they won the pennant.

[2] MacPhail sold his share of the team after the 1947 season.

[3] Huston sold his share of the team to Ruppert in 1922.

THE HOUSE THAT LINDSAY REBUILT

The New Jersey Yankees? By the early 1970s, the architectural majesty of Yankee Stadium was fading and its Bronx neighborhood was becoming more run-down. At the same time, the team had become mediocre and attendance had dwindled. Team president Michael Burke threatened to move the team to the new Meadowlands sports complex across the river if the city didn't do something to fix the aging stadium.

Although New York City was on the brink of financial ruin—its plight immortalized in the 1975 *New York Daily News* headline: "[President] Ford to City: Drop Dead"—Mayor John Lindsay agreed to finance what he thought would be a $24 million facelift.

He was a little off. A massive two-year reconstruction of the stadium, which also forced the Yankees to play their 1974 and 1975 home games in Shea Stadium, would eventually cost a whopping $167 million of public money.

By then, George Steinbrenner had arrived. His Yankees—and Yankee Stadium—would never be the same. The renovated stadium (a.k.a. "The House That Lindsay Rebuilt") was a different place, both visually and structurally. Gone was Death Valley as the fences were moved in considerably. Also gone were the center field monuments and plaques, two-thirds of the bleacher seats, and the distinctive frieze that had ringed the original roof.

View-obstructing support poles were also removed. Escalators to the upper decks and wider seats were installed. Roads leading to the stadium were improved. And it wasn't hard to find the world's largest Louisville Slugger, a 138-foot smokestack that sprang up by the main entrance. The bat became a meeting place for fans, and there would be a lot more fans.

The remodeled stadium was opened and rededicated on April 15, 1976, to much fanfare.

1974–1975 renovation

Mrs. Babe Ruth, Mrs. Lou Gehrig, and Joe Louis were among the numerous luminaries on hand. Eighty-five-year-old Bob Shawkey, who pitched a three-hitter when Yankee Stadium opened in 1923, threw out the first pitch.

So began a new era of Yankee baseball. With the new stadium and Steinbrenner's spending policy—the Boss aggressively played the free-agent market—the Yankees drew 2,012,434 fans during the 1976 regular season. They were the first American League team to draw more than two million since they'd done it themselves a quarter-century earlier.

On October 14, 1976, the Stadium hosted one of the most supercharged moments in Yankee history. Chris Chambliss's ninth-inning home run against the Kansas City Royals gave the team their first pennant in 12 seasons and set off a chaotic celebration as hundreds of fans stormed the field.

Excitement certainly returned with the modernized stadium, but more than a few people left their hearts in the old place. "When I first came to Yankee Stadium I used to feel like the ghosts of Babe Ruth and Lou Gehrig were walking around in there," said Mickey Mantle. "After they remodeled Yankee Stadium, I didn't feel that the ghosts were there anymore. It just wasn't the same."

Have faith in the Yankees, my son.

—ERNEST HEMINGWAY IN HIS 1952 NOVEL, *THE OLD MAN AND THE SEA*

DESIGNATED HISTORY

On Opening Day in 1973, a free spirit named Ron Blomberg drew a bases-loaded, first-inning walk from Boston's Luis Tiant. It was the first time a designated hitter was used in a game since the American League implemented the new rule. It was a big deal, but not to Blomberg. "I've been a DH all my life," he said. "Designated Hebrew."

CHAIRMAN OF THE BOARD

Edward Charles "Whitey" Ford stood only 5′10″, but he rose to the challenge in big games. During the 1950s and early '60s, the savvy lefty made winning World Series games a virtual habit. He once threw a record 33⅔ consecutive scoreless World Series innings. Ford, known as Chairman of the Board for his impeccable efficiency and control, is the greatest Yankee pitcher of all time. His career record is 236–106 with a 2.74 ERA. His winning percentage of .690 is the greatest of any pitcher in the 20th century.

Like fellow Yankee legends Lou Gehrig and Phil Rizzuto, Whitey was born in New York City. He was the son of working-class parents in Astoria, Queens. He debuted with the Yankees midway through the 1950 season, winning nine of ten decisions. Ford then missed the next two seasons because of military service. When he returned, he became the team's unquestioned ace until his retirement in 1967. As his longtime pal and teammate Mickey Mantle once said, "I don't care what the situation was, how high the stakes were—the bases could be loaded and the pennant riding on every pitch, it never bothered Whitey Ford. He pitched his game. Cool. Crafty. Nerves of steel."

"BABE was no ordinary man. He was not alone the IDOL of the fans; he was a SUPERMAN to the ballplayers. Ruth possessed a MAGNETISM that was positively infectious. When he entered a clubhouse or a room, when he appeared on a field, it was as if he was the whole PARADE. There seemed to be flags waving, bands playing constantly."

—Hall of Fame pitcher Waite Hoyt, Ruth's teammate from 1921 to 1930

NO-NO, NO-NO ALLIE

Before Joba Chamberlain, there was Allie Reynolds. He was another hard-throwing, part Native American right-hander. Reynolds—known as Superchief—won 131 games during his Yankee career (1947–1954). Few were more memorable than his two no-hitters in 1951.

The first was a 1–0 victory on July 12, against the Cleveland Indians and Bob Feller, who had pitched his own no-hitter 11 days earlier. The second was an 8–0 victory on September 28, against the Boston Red Sox, which ended in high drama.

With two outs in the ninth, Reynolds had to face Ted Williams, the greatest hitter in baseball history. Williams hit a towering pop foul, and catcher Yogi Berra drifted under it—and dropped it.

Reynolds rushed over to his despondent catcher and told him not to worry. On the next pitch, Williams popped it up again. This time, Berra, with Reynolds at his side, grabbed it. The win clinched a tie for the pennant and made Reynolds just the second pitcher in baseball history to deliver two no-hitters in one season.

Yankee Final Resting Places

Joe DiMaggio Holy Cross Cemetery, Colma, California

Lou Gehrig Kensico Cemetery, Valhalla, New York

Catfish Hunter Cedarwood Cemetery, Hertford, North Carolina

Mickey Mantle Sparkman-Hillcrest Memorial Park Cemetery, Dallas, Texas

Roger Maris Holy Cross Cemetery, Fargo, North Dakota

Billy Martin Gate of Heaven Cemetery, Hawthorne, New York

Thurman Munson Sunset Hills Burial Park, Canton, Ohio

Babe Ruth Gate of Heaven Cemetery, Hawthorne, New York

Casey Stengel Forest Lawn Cemetery, Glendale, California

Babe Ruth's grave

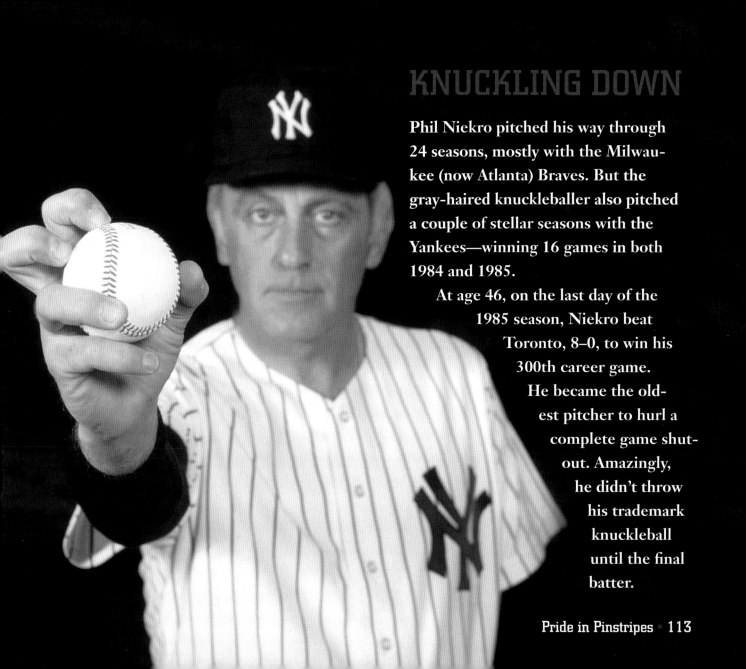

KNUCKLING DOWN

Phil Niekro pitched his way through 24 seasons, mostly with the Milwaukee (now Atlanta) Braves. But the gray-haired knuckleballer also pitched a couple of stellar seasons with the Yankees—winning 16 games in both 1984 and 1985.

At age 46, on the last day of the 1985 season, Niekro beat Toronto, 8–0, to win his 300th career game. He became the oldest pitcher to hurl a complete game shutout. Amazingly, he didn't throw his trademark knuckleball until the final batter.

BATTLIN' BILLY

Billy Martin argues with umpires.

Alfred Manuel "Billy" Martin had a little temper. He was a scrappy Yankee second baseman in the 1950s who was deemed a troublemaker by the management. Indeed, he never minded mixing it up. This was especially true during his brawling managerial career, which included five stints with the Yankees. In his first dugout job with Minnesota in 1969, he knocked out one of his pitchers. He also punched the traveling secretaries of both the Twins and Rangers while managing for those teams. Martin suffered a broken arm in a fight with Ed Whitson, one of his Yankee pitchers, and also beat up a marshmallow salesman in 1979.

MANAGERIAL RECORD WITH YANKEES
1975–1979, 1983, 1985, 1988
WINS: 556
LOSSES: 385
WIN PERCENTAGE: .591
PENNANTS: 2
CHAMPIONSHIPS: 1

"This team could never have become what it did without BILLY MARTIN managing it. Billy had that FIERINESS. He had that COMPETITIVENESS that oozed all over him."

—Sparky Lyle in his 1979 book, *The Bronx Zoo*

DiMAG'S DEBUT

No other Yankee made a rookie splash quite like Joe DiMaggio. In 1936, Joltin' Joe batted .323 with 125 RBI and 29 homers, all club rookie records. His 132 runs scored remains an American League rookie record.

Derek Jeter

Yankee Rookies of the Year
AWARD INSTITUTED IN 1947

1951: Gil McDougald
Batted .306, primarily played third base

1954: Bob Grim
Right-hander went 20–6 with a 3.26 ERA

1957: Tony Kubek
Played outfield, third, and shortstop, and batted .297

1962: Tom Tresh
Shortstop hit .286 with 20 homers

1968: Stan Bahnsen
Right-hander went 17–12 with a 2.05 ERA

1970: Thurman Munson
Played 125 games as catcher and hit .302

1981: Dave Righetti
Lefty starter went 8–4 with a 2.05 ERA

1996: Derek Jeter
Shortstop hit .314 for the first championship team in 18 years

Notable Yankee Openers

1923: **Babe Ruth** baptizes the new $2.5 million Yankee Stadium with a home run. A crowd of 74,000 sees the Yankees beat the Red Sox 4–1.

1939: Rookie **Ted Williams** debuts as Boston loses to the Yankees 2–0. It's the only game in which Williams and Lou Gehrig ever appear together.

1950: The Yankees rally from a 9–0 deficit in Fenway Park to win 15–10. **Billy Martin** is the first rookie to get two hits in one inning.

1955: The Yankees trounce Washington, 19–1, at Yankee Stadium in the most lopsided Opening Day victory in history.

1960: **Roger Maris** hits two homers in his Yankee debut, an 8–4 victory over Boston at Fenway Park.

1975: Cleveland's **Frank Robinson** debuts as baseball's first black manager and hits a home run to lead his team to a 5–3 victory over the Yankees.

1998: On the 75th anniversary season of Yankee Stadium, the Yankees hold off Oakland, 17–13.

2004: The Yankees lose to Tampa Bay, 8–3, in Tokyo, as ex-Yankee **Tino Martinez** homers against his former club.

Yankee No-Hitters

George Mogridge: April 24, 1917

Sam Jones: September 4, 1923

Monte Pearson: August 27, 1938

Allie Reynolds: July 12, 1951

Allie Reynolds: September 28, 1951

Don Larsen: October 8, 1956

Dave Righetti: July 4, 1983

Andy Hawkins: July 1, 1990

Jim Abbott: September 4, 1993

Dwight Gooden: May 14, 1996

David Wells: May 17, 1996

David Cone: July 18, 1999

Dave Righetti

THE VOICE OF GOD

"Your attention please, ladies and gentlemen. Now batting for the Yankees...."
For nearly 60 years, Bob Sheppard has been the official, uniquely elegant voice of Yankee Stadium and a beloved treasure. He is more than just a public address announcer; he is an institution. The man and his voice are as distinguished and distinctive as Yankee pinstripes or the stadium frieze.

Sheppard is a former professor of speech at St. John's University, and his unmistakable sound—which Reggie Jackson dubbed "the voice of God"—became part of the Yankee Stadium atmosphere beginning in 1951. He also became the public address announcer for New York Giants football games and for many other non-Yankee events. But his announcing for the Yankees is what made him world-famous.

Bob Sheppard

Public address announcers are usually anonymous, but Bob Sheppard is hardly that. He has been called upon to write tributes, and he delivered a moving eulogy to the victims of the September 11 attacks. Fittingly, he has a plaque in Monument Park.

FAMOUS FAREWELLS

In two grim, emotional appearances, the immortal duo of Babe Ruth and Lou Gehrig said their respective goodbyes at Yankee Stadium. On July 4, 1939, Gehrig, diagnosed with an incurable disease, gave his moving "luckiest man" speech and died less than two years later at age 37. On June 13, 1948, Ruth, stricken with cancer and wearing a heavy camel's hair coat, praised his sport and thanked the fans for supporting him. He died two months later at age 53.

Paul O'Neill is no immortal. But the retiring outfielder got an unforgettable farewell tribute from Yankee fans, who serenaded him with chants of "Paul O'Neill! Paul O'Neill! Paul O'Neill!" in Game 5 of the 2001 World Series.

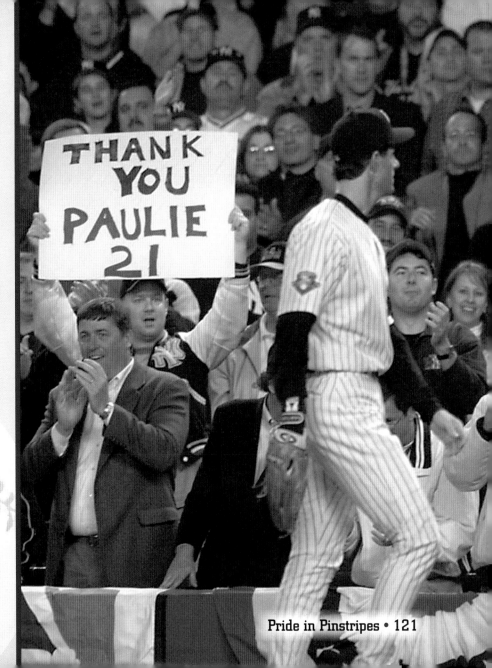

YANKEES ABC's

J Jeter

This cool, confident, classy captain of the
Yankees has been the handsome face of the
franchise since 1996. A quiet leader, Derek
Sanderson Jeter has been called the
DiMaggio of his generation. He wears
No. 2, but he's No. 1 in the hearts of leg-
ions of Yankee fans, both young and old.

K "King Kong" Keller

Charlie Keller, a powerful left fielder of
the 1940s, was nicknamed after the famous
movie ape because of his bushy eyebrows
and brute strength. At just 5′10″ and
185 pounds, he was no giant, but he was
one of the strongest players and greatest
hustlers of his era.

Charlie "King Kong" Keller

L Lou Gehrig

How many people dying of an incurable disease could say, "I consider myself the luckiest man on the face of the earth?" Henry Louis Gehrig's humility and courage knew no bounds. He was the greatest first baseman in the game's history, but his incredible work ethic and rare courage made him an idol for the ages.

M M&M Boys

Mickey Mantle and Roger Maris captivated the nation in 1961 with their pursuit of Babe Ruth's single-season home run record. The press gave Mantle and Maris the double-M nickname and tried to portray a feud between the sluggers, but to no avail.

Maris and Mantle

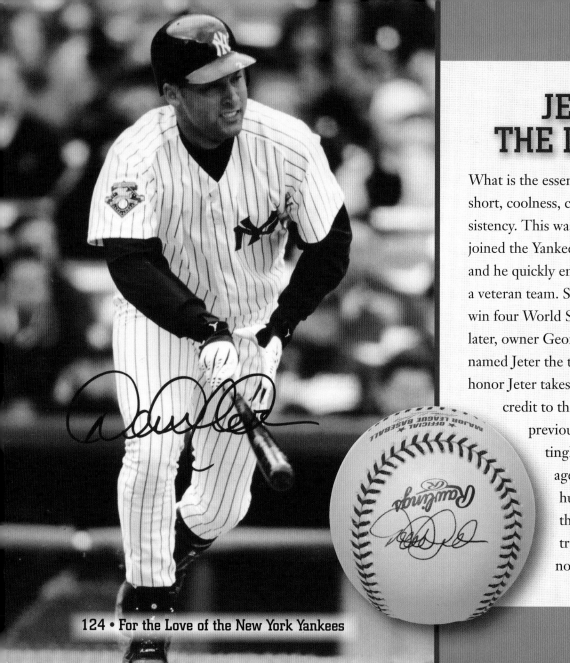

JETER THE LEADER

What is the essence of Derek Jeter? In short, coolness, confidence, and consistency. This was apparent when he joined the Yankees in 1995 at age 21, and he quickly emerged as a leader on a veteran team. Soon, that team would win four World Series. Seven years later, owner George Steinbrenner named Jeter the team's captain, an honor Jeter takes seriously. He gives credit to the advice of the team's previous captain, Don Mattingly, who once encouraged the young Jeter to hustle, not walk, across the field of a spring-training game, even if nobody was watching.

Yankee Captains

YEARS	PLAYER	POSITION
1912	Hal Chase	1B
1914–1921	Roger Peckinpaugh	SS
1922	Babe Ruth*	OF
1922–1925	Everett Scott	SS
1935–1941	Lou Gehrig	1B
1976–1979	Thurman Munson	C
1982–1983	Graig Nettles	3B
1986–1989	Ron Guidry**	P
1986–1989	Willie Randolph**	2B
1991–1995	Don Mattingly	1B
2003–present	Derek Jeter	SS

* Captain for six days
** Co-captains

Best Yankee Third Basemen

Alex Rodriguez (2004–present)
Currently, the game's biggest superstar

Graig Nettles (1973–1983)
Power bat and great glove contributed to titles in the late '70s

Red Rolfe (1931, 1934–1942)
Clutch performer on six pennant-winning teams

Wade Boggs (1993–1997)
Hall of Fame hitter, won two Gold Gloves as a Yankee

Clete Boyer (1959–1966)
Flawless defender on powerhouse teams of the early '60s

Clete Boyer

CLASSIC NETTLES

After legendary Oriole third baseman Brooks Robinson retired, Graig Nettles finally got the attention he deserved at the position. In 1977 and 1978, the Yankees' acrobatic cornerman captured two Gold Gloves and played magnificently before a national audience in the World Series against the Dodgers.

THE MADNESS OF KING GEORGE

George Steinbrenner was born in a town called Rocky River—honest. Of course, in his always-interesting, 35-year ownership of the Yankees, he's hit more than a few bumps. But he's also put the team on a path to glory. Before the 2008 season, the Boss handed the reins of the franchise over to his sons Hank and Hal.

So how will Boisterous George be remembered? On the one hand, Steinbrenner was demanding and driven, as well as generous and giving. On the other hand, he could be impulsive, bombastic, and also a bully and a tyrant.

He was twice suspended from baseball. At one point, he hired a small-time gambler to dig up dirt on star player Dave Winfield, whom he sarcastically called "Mr. May." In addition, Steinbrenner almost went off the deep end in 1981, when he fired manager Gene Michael with only 25 games left in the season. Another time, he humiliated Reggie Jackson by ordering him to take eye tests. During the 1981 World Series, he

broke his hand in an alleged fight with Dodger fans in an elevator. When the Yankees lost the Series, he apologized to the City of New York, guaranteeing it would never happen again.

In spite of all the theatrics, this much we know: There will never be another George Steinbrenner.

Steinbrenner with New York Governor George Pataki

"We plan absentee ownership as far as running the YANKEES is concerned. We're not going to pretend we're something we're not. I'll stick to building ships."

—GEORGE STEINBRENNER AT THE 1973 PRESS CONFERENCE ANNOUNCING HIS PURCHASE OF THE YANKEES

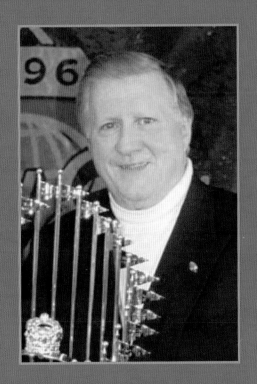

SEE YA

"See ya" is Yankee broadcaster Michael Kay's call for a home run. In 1956, it might have been a more direct way of telling two players they were now ex-Yankees.

Before a game, Casey Stengel walked into the Yankee dugout and said, "Nobody knows this but one of us has been traded to Kansas City." Reserve outfielder Bob Cerv was the only player sitting there. He got the message. However, the trade was delayed and he didn't report to Kansas City until the season ended. Cerv would later return for two more stints with the Yankees.

One month later, on Old-Timers' Day, ironically, the Yankees acquired 40-year-old Enos Slaughter from the Kansas City A's to help with the pennant race. Thirty-nine-year-old short-stop Phil Rizzuto was summoned to meet with George Weiss and Casey Stengel for his suggestions on which player to release to make room

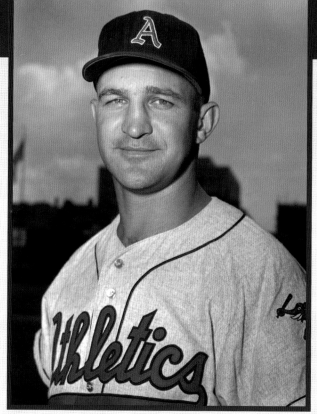

Bob Cerv after his trade to Kansas City

for Slaughter. Rizzuto gave a few names, but then it dawned on him that he was being set up. The Scooter, who had been the anchor of the Yankee infield since joining the team in 1941, was the player being released.

OLD COUNTRY

Enos "Country" Slaughter played in more than 1,800 games with the Cardinals. By the time he was traded to the Yankees in 1954, he was an aging player. Still, the old man batted .350 in the 1956 World Series. Two years later, at age 42, he led the league in pinch-hit at-bats and batted .304.

THE CATCHING TRADITION

Catcher is a grueling and punishing position, but it's also a crucial position that requires strategy and leadership. Fortunately, the Yankees have been blessed with a tradition of catching excellence that dates back to 1929.

That's when a tall, rangy, 22-year-old named Bill Dickey became the team's full-time backstop. By the time he hung up his mask in 1946, he was an all-time great. Dickey hit .300 or better in 11 seasons—including a career-high .362 in 1936, the highest of any major-league catcher—and handled the pitching staff like a maestro.

His defensive influence would live on with the Yankees for another generation. In 1949, new manager Casey Stengel summoned Dickey out of retirement to tutor a raw, scatter-armed catcher named Yogi Berra. Dickey worked tirelessly to teach the fine points of catching to Berra, who always credited Dickey for "learning me all his experience." Berra would go on to win three Most Valuable Player awards and handle a record 950 straight chances without an error.

Bill Dickey

By the mid-1950s, Dickey, then a Yankee coach, mentored Elston Howard, the team's first African American player, who gradually got more time behind the plate as Berra was phased into the outfield. Howard became a standout all-around catcher, hitting .348 in 1961 and winning league MVP honors in 1963.

The catching tradition continued with the emergence of squatty Thurman Munson, who won Rookie of the Year honors in 1970. Because of the Billy-George-Reggie theatrics of the Yankee teams in the late '70s, Munson's leadership and accomplishments were sometimes overlooked. Still, he won league MVP in 1976, three Gold Gloves, and became a seven-time All-Star before his untimely death at age 32 in 1979.

Since becoming a Yankee regular in the late 1990s, switch-hitting Jorge Posada has been extremely respectful of the Yankee catcher tradition. He has formed a close friendship with

Thurman Munson

Berra, whom he tied in 2003 for most single-season homers by a Yankee catcher (30). Posada also seems to be getting better with age, hitting a career-high .338 at age 36 in 2007.

MICK THE QUICK

Yankee center fielder Mickey Rivers was known as much for his quick wit as his playing.

"To hit .300, score 100 runs, and stay injury-prone."

—ON HIS GOALS FOR THE 1983 SEASON,
QUOTED IN THE *St. Petersburg Times*, MARCH 30, 1983

"Out of what? A thousand?"

—ON HEARING REGGIE JACKSON BRAG ABOUT HAVING AN IQ OF 160

"Me and George and Billy are two of a kind."

—ON DENYING HE'D HAVE ANY TROUBLE WITH GEORGE STEINBRENNER
OR BILLY MARTIN IF HE WENT BACK TO THE YANKEES, QUOTED IN
Sports Illustrated, MARCH 28, 1983

ST. JOE

"*Joe understood the bargain **PERFECTLY**. He understood the bargain with **PERFECTION**. He could have our honor, our adulation, the glory of the Big Name.... He understood: we would give him anything— if he would be the hero we required.*"

—RICHARD BEN CRAMER IN THE BOOK *JOE DIMAGGIO: THE HERO'S LIFE*

REMEMBERING THURMAN

During 1970 spring training, a gruff, tough kid from Ohio named Thurman Munson won the Yankee's starting catcher job. He became the take-charge guy in the Yankees' return to glory and the backbone of the 1977 and 1978 world championship teams. When Munson died tragically in a plane crash at age 32, his teammates and fans were numb for weeks. In all the years since his death, his locker has never been given to another player. It remains empty to this day.

"*Someone, some day, shall earn that right to lead this team again. For that is how* THURM *would want it. And that is how one day it will be. No* GREATER HONOR *could be bestowed upon one man than to be the successor to this man....*"

—BOBBY MURCER IN HIS EULOGY TO TEAMMATE AND CAPTAIN THURMAN MUNSON, WHOSE LIFE WAS TRAGICALLY CUT SHORT ON AUGUST 2, 1979

BROTHERS IN PINSTRIPES

The new bosses—Hank and Hal Steinbrenner—aren't the only brothers in Yankee history.

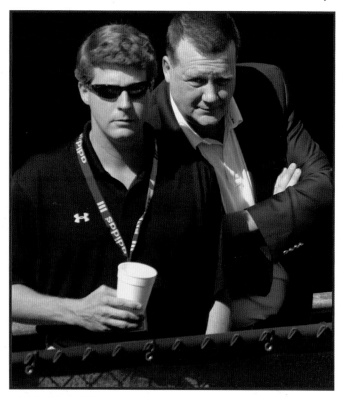

Hal (left) and Hank Steinbrenner

- In 1912, Tommy and Homer Thompson briefly played for the New York Highlanders.
- Bobby Shantz pitched for the Yankees from 1957 to 1960, and his brother Billy, a catcher, played one game for the 1960 Yankees.
- Matty and Felipe Alou played together as Yankees in 1973. They also played together against the Yankees in the 1962 World Series when they were with San Francisco.
- Pitcher Joe Niekro was reunited with his older brother Phil when both played for the Yankees in 1985.
- Pascual Perez pitched unremarkably for the Yankees from 1990 to 1991, and his brother Melido did the same from 1992 to 1995.
- Al Leiter started and ended his long pitching career with the Yankees but wasn't on the team when his brother Mark pitched eight games for them in 1990.

OH, BOYER

**CLETE and KEN BOYER, two of 14 children, were supreme
third basemen who made history in the 1964 World Series.
Clete (Yankees) and Ken (Cardinals) became the first brothers
to hit home runs for opposing teams in a World Series game.**

ELEMENTARY, WATSON

Bob Watson had a distinguished 19-year career. He ended with a .295 average and will always be remembered for scoring baseball's one-millionth run in 1975. Also, Watson was the first man to hit for the cycle in both the American and National Leagues.

Yet what Watson did off the field was downright trailblazing. The determined, intelligent man known as "Bull" broke a longstanding barrier by becoming the game's first African American general manager when he took over the Astros in 1994. A few months later, he learned he had prostate cancer, but he was able to beat the disease.

Two years later, Watson became vice president and general manager of the Yankees, a team he'd played on from 1980 to 1982. The team hadn't won a world championship in 18 years. Somehow, he kept George Steinbrenner, the world's most meddlesome owner, at bay. Watson added all the right pieces and helped instill a team-first attitude for the boys in pinstripes. His hard work resulted in the 1996 world championship and the beginning of a brand-new dynasty for the Yankees.

Watson didn't stick around for long. In February 1998, with high blood pressure and worries about being "burned out," he resigned. Yet he made another right move by pushing for the promotion of his 30-year-old assistant, Brian Cashman, to succeed him.

Bob Watson during his early-'80s stint with the Yankees

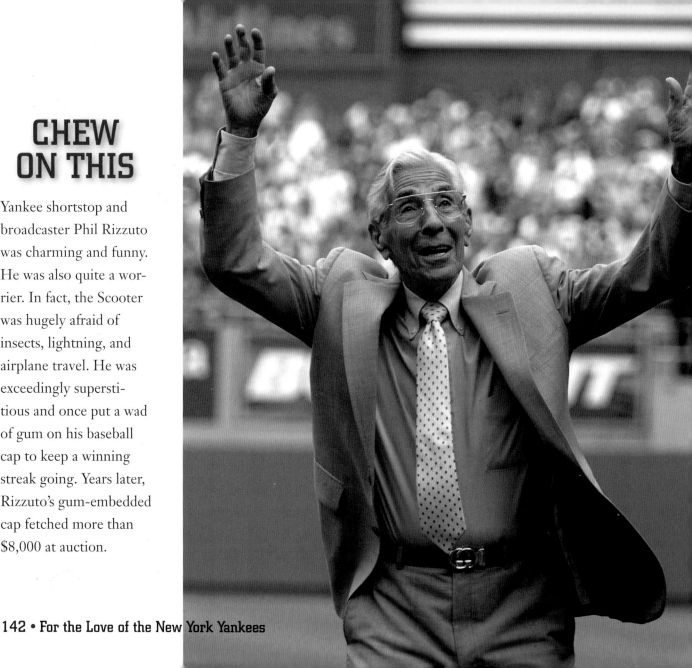

CHEW ON THIS

Yankee shortstop and broadcaster Phil Rizzuto was charming and funny. He was also quite a worrier. In fact, the Scooter was hugely afraid of insects, lightning, and airplane travel. He was exceedingly superstitious and once put a wad of gum on his baseball cap to keep a winning streak going. Years later, Rizzuto's gum-embedded cap fetched more than $8,000 at auction.

> *I only have one. I touch all the bases when I hit a home run.*
>
> —BABE RUTH ON SUPERSTITIONS

YANKEE SUPERSTITIONS

Superstitions are an integral part of baseball. Here are some notable Yankee superstitions:

- Wade Boggs, a man of many superstitions, ate chicken before each game and drew a chai—the Hebrew sign for life—in the batter's box before each at-bat.
- Lefty O'Doul skipped over the baseline to and from the pitcher's mound.
- **Roger Clemens touched Babe Ruth's plaque in Monument Park before he pitched.**
- Mike Pagliarulo wore a red ribbon in his underwear to keep evil away.
- George Steinbrenner stood in the same spot in the owner's box if the Yankees were winning.

The 1961 Yankees

SUMMER OF '61

When you think 1961 Yankees, you can't help but think M&M Boys. Here's something else to think about: The Yankees were an incredible 65–16 (.802) at home that season. They hit 240 home runs, and their three catchers—Yogi Berra, Elston Howard, and Johnny Blanchard—each hit more than 20 homers apiece.

On the pitching side of the game, Whitey Ford won the Cy Young Award with a 25–4 record. Luis Arroyo led the league with 29 saves. Defensively, their infield, which featured Moose Skowron, Bobby Richardson, Tony Kubek, and Clete Boyer, was the best in the game.

Greatest Yankee Teams

YEAR	W–L	PCT.	MGR.	WON DIVISION BY
1927	110–44	.714	Huggins	19 games
1998	114–48	.704	Torre	22 games
1939	106–45	.702	McCarthy	17 games
1961	109–53	.673	Houk	8 games
1936	102–51	.667	McCarthy	19.5 games
1953	99–52	.656	Stengel	8.5 games

Joe Torre

CHAPTER FOUR

YANKEE-PANKY

"*I came into this game sane, and I want to leave it sane.*"

—Don Baylor, on why he would say no if George Steinbrenner offered him the job of Yankee manager, *Sports Illustrated*, October 19, 1987

Don Zimmer following his moment of insanity with Pedro Martinez

RAINING REGGIES

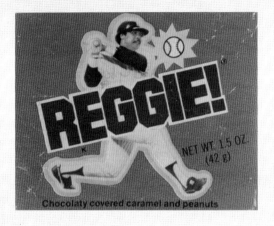

Reggie Jackson always said if he played in New York "they'd have a candy bar for me." They surely did. On April 13, 1978, the Yankees staged a promotion by giving away Reggie Bars, a brand-new, 25-cent glob of chocolate and peanuts. Showman that he was, Jackson homered against the White Sox, prompting fans to fling thousands of Reggie Bars at their self-promoting hero. "People starving all over the world and 30 billion calories are laying on the field," groused Sox manager Bob Lemon.

STIRRING IT UP

*I'm the straw
that stirs
the drink.*
**[Thurman] Munson
thinks he can be the
straw that stirs the
drink, but he can
only stir it bad.**"

—REGGIE JACKSON IN HIS INFAMOUS
1977 *SPORT* MAGAZINE INTERVIEW

Youse from Brooklyn?

Brooklyn is famous for the Brooklyn Bridge, the Brooklyn Dodgers, and Nathan's Famous hot dogs. It's also where some Yankees were born or raised. Here are a few Yankees from Brooklyn:

Joe Pepitone

Willie Randolph

Phil Rizzuto

Marius Russo

Joe Torre

NOW HAIR THIS

Joe Pepitone, a wild and crazy Yankee in the 1960s, was known for his interesting hair, which he embellished with a hairpiece. Notably, he was the first major-league player to have a hair dryer in the clubhouse. Pepi also owned a salon for men called My Place.

Bobby Richardson

Tony Kubek

MILKSHAKE TWINS

Some of the Yankees of the 1950s, notably Mickey Mantle and Whitey Ford, liked the nightlife so much that the team's management hired detectives to follow them. For some reason, the detectives once followed Bobby Richardson and Tony Kubek, the team's double-play combo and a pair of super-straight arrows.

That night, Richardson and Kubek were on their way to a local YMCA for a table tennis tournament. Both bought popcorn and had a milkshake. They were dubbed the Milkshake Twins and are still known as such.

Hank Bauer, Mickey Mantle, and Gene Woodling

"Don't mess with my money!"

—HANK BAUER TO ANY TEAMMATE HE THOUGHT WASN'T GIVING MAXIMUM
EFFORT, SINCE IT MIGHT JEOPARDIZE HIS WORLD SERIES CHECK

PINE-TARRED AND FEATHERED

Possibly the stickiest incident in Yankee history occurred on July 24, 1983, when George Brett hit a dramatic two-run homer off Goose Gossage to give the Kansas City Royals a 5–4 lead in the ninth inning at Yankee Stadium.

As Brett happily rounded the bases, Yankee manager Billy Martin hatched a unique plan. He convinced the umpires to disallow the homer—citing an obscure rule prohibiting pine tar from extending more than 18 inches on a bat. Brett's bat exceeded that limit, so the Yankees won!

Brett's dislike for the Yankees was intense, and having a homer taken away made him insanely angry. Screaming and waving his arms like a man gone berserk, he nearly ran over umpire Tim McClelland in protest, and it took a rugby scrum to pull him away. "The sight of George coming out of the dugout is etched in my mind forever," Don Mattingly said years later.

But the Yankees' apparent 4–3 victory didn't last. American League president Lee MacPhail upheld the Royals' protest, and the game was resumed 21 days later at Yankee Stadium, with the Royals leading 5–4 and two outs in the top of the ninth. This time the Yankees lost, which didn't please a different George—a blustery chap named Steinbrenner—who suggested MacPhail move to Kansas City for his own safety.

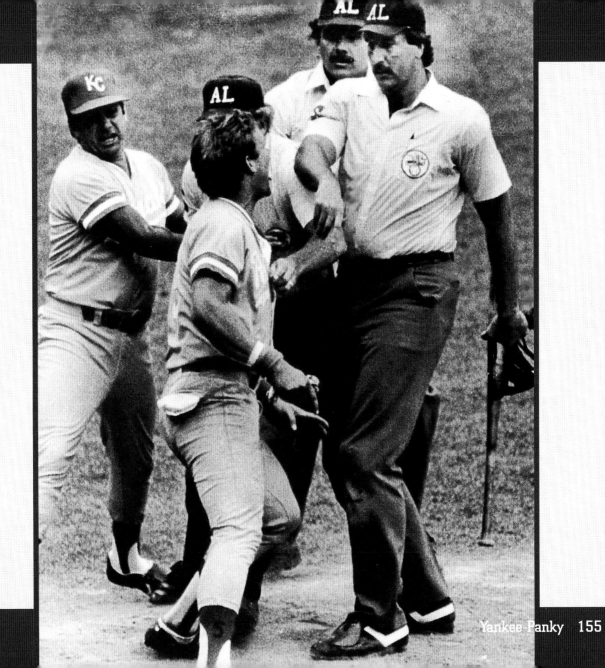

Jose Contreras

WORST *Yankee* TRADES

December 9, 1941 Traded Tommy Holmes to the Boston Braves for Buddy Hassett and Gene Moore. Holmes, the only player to lead the league in home runs and fewest strikeouts, had a stellar post-Yankee career.

October 21, 1981 Traded Willie McGee to the St. Louis Cardinals for Bob Sykes. Switch-hitting speedster McGee later won two batting titles.

December 9, 1982 Traded Dave Collins, Fred McGriff, Mike Morgan, and cash to the Toronto Blue Jays for Dale Murray and Tom Dodd. McGriff wound up hitting 493 career homers. Trading McGriff the Crime Dog was criminal.

July 21, 1988 Traded Jay Buhner, Rich Balabon, and Troy Evers to the Seattle Mariners for Ken Phelps. As Frank Costanza said on *Seinfeld*, "What the hell did you trade Jay Buhner for?"

July 31, 2004 Traded Jose Contreras to the Chicago White Sox for Esteban Loaiza. The Cuban righty became the ace of the Sox's first championship in 88 years.

DUGOUT DEBACLE

In 1977, the year the Bronx burned, nobody got more incensed than fiery Billy Martin. And never was that more apparent than during the nationally televised June 18 game at Fenway Park.

Martin was a hustle player during his entire career and demanded nothing less from the players he managed. So he fumed when his star, Reggie Jackson, loafed during a soft hit, which Boston's Jim Rice turned into a cheap double. Martin immediately yanked his sensitive slugger out of the game, and the fun began.

"What's going on?" Jackson screamed at Martin in the dugout. "What did I do?"

"You didn't hustle," Martin shouted back.

"You have to be crazy to embarrass me in front of 50 million people," Jackson yelled. "You're not a man. Don't you ever show me up again, you [expletive]."

Martin charged at Jackson but was forcibly restrained by coaches Elston Howard and Yogi Berra. Among the millions of viewers who witnessed the dugout debacle was a guy in Cleveland—owner George Steinbrenner. He reportedly ordered Martin's firing on the spot but relented after haggling with team president, Gabe Paul. Four months later, Billy and Reggie were at each other's necks again—hugging after winning the World Series.

Martin and Jackson make nice.

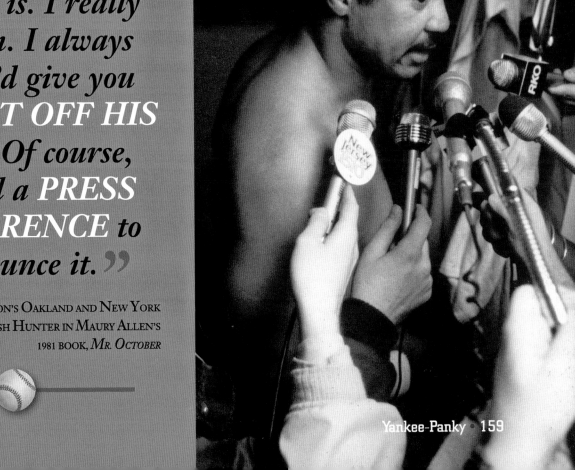

> *"Reggie's really a **GOOD GUY**; deep down he is. I really like him. I always did. He'd give you the **SHIRT OFF HIS BACK**. Of course, he'd call a **PRESS CONFERENCE** to announce it."*

—Reggie Jackson's Oakland and New York teammate Catfish Hunter in Maury Allen's 1981 book, *Mr. October*

YANKEES ABC's

N *No, No Nanette*

This lighthearted Broadway production left Boston Red Sox owner (and theater impresario) Harry Frazee in need of money in 1919. Frazee sold off a 24-year-old pitcher/outfielder named Babe Ruth to the Yankees for $125,000. The good news for Frazee is that *No, No Nanette*, which didn't open until 1925, became a hit. The Babe was kind of a hit, too.

O Osborn Engineering Company

This Cleveland company—the same firm that built Fenway and Comiskey—was the architect of Yankee Stadium. Osborn designed the king of all baseball stadiums with a capacity of 70,000, nearly twice that of any park at the time. Yankee Stadium was built in an incredible 284 days at a total cost of $2.5 million.

P Pinstripes

The pinstripes have been part of the Yankee uniform since 1912. The Yankee pinstripe uniform is one of the classiest designs in any sport. For years, many believed that the Yankees adopted pinstripes to make the portly Babe Ruth look more svelte. This is simply a myth. In truth, the basic Yankee uniform hasn't changed in more than 90 years.

Q Quick

This is the nickname for Mickey Rivers, perhaps the fleetest man to ever play for the Yankees. Mick the Quick was the offensive catalyst of the late 1970s teams, and he covered lots of ground in center field. He was also quick to notice that Bucky Dent had a crack in his bat when facing Mike Torrez in the famed 1978 playoff game. So he lent Dent one of his, and the light-hitting shortstop hit his improbable home run.

Mickey Rivers

THE ROARING REDHEAD

Larry MacPhail—the Roaring Redhead—ran the Yankees for three years (1945–1947), and it was seldom dull. He was a loud man who created plenty of excitement. In 1946, he installed lights at Yankee Stadium and saw attendance soar to a major-league record of 2.3 million.

But in 1947, he became Crazy Larry, fighting with anyone at any time. Moments after the Yankees beat the Dodgers in the World Series, MacPhail, waving a beer bottle during his team's celebration, roared, "That's my retirement!" And manic MacPhail left the building.

FOLLY FLOATER

Steve Hamilton, who pitched for the Yankees from 1963 to 1970, occasionally used to lob a pitch that went up, up, and up, and then came down, down, and down. The left-hander described the pitch as a "gag," but it was better known as the Folly Floater.

Steve Hamilton with his son, Bobby

RICKEY BEING RICKEY

There's never been a better leadoff hitter than Rickey Henderson, baseball's all-time leader in runs and stolen bases. Rickey certainly left his mark on the Yankees during his years with the team (1985–1989). He still holds the team's single-season stolen base record with 93 in 1988. Henderson often held court with reporters, talking about himself in the third person and referring to his constant "hammy," or hamstring, injuries. And Rickey kept his teammates amused, once telling them his condo had such a great view that he could see "the Entire State Building."

YANKEE LEAGUE LEADERS IN STOLEN BASES

2002 Alfonso Soriano (41)

1989 Rickey Henderson (77)*

1988 Rickey Henderson (93)

1986 Rickey Henderson (87)

1985 Rickey Henderson (80)

1945 Snuffy Stirnweiss (33)

1944 Snuffy Stirnweiss (55)

1938 Frank Crosetti (27)

1933 Ben Chapman (27)

1932 Ben Chapman (38)

1931 Ben Chapman (61)

1914 Fritz Maisel (74)

* includes half-season with Oakland

THE COPA

This legend of the Copacabana has nothing to do with pop singer Barry Manilow or his yellow-feathered showgirl, Lola. Make no mistake, the famous New York nightclub was the scene of the most infamous brawl in Yankee history.

On May 16, 1957, six players were celebrating Billy Martin's 29th birthday by checking out

Mantle, Martin, and Hank and Charlene Bauer following a court appearance stemming from the Copa incident

Sammy Davis, Jr., at the Copa. At a nearby table was a group of bowlers, one of whom shouted racial insults at Davis. Hank Bauer, a former Marine, took special exception to this. It's still unclear what happened next, except that one of the bowlers was knocked unconscious in the restroom. The Yankees claimed a bouncer punched him.

Unfortunately for the players—Bauer, Martin, Mickey Mantle, Whitey Ford, Yogi Berra, and Johnny Kucks—gossip columnist Leonard Lyons was there and interviewed the bowlers. The Copa incident became splashy front-page news.

While the Yankees maintained their innocence, someone had to pay. GM George Weiss, who expected his players to behave like Boy Scouts, fined each player $1,000, a substantial amount in those days. Martin, who by all accounts was well behaved that night, got the worst punishment. Weiss blamed him for the trouble, and a month later he was traded to Kansas City.

"They got on *BILLY* later for being a *BAD INFLUENCE* on Mickey and traded him. They said he was a bad influence on all the guys. All I know is the year he roomed with me, I was the MVP, the year he roomed with Yogi, he was the MVP, and the year he roomed with Mickey, he was the MVP. Some bad influence."

—PHIL RIZZUTO IN MAURY ALLEN'S 1979 BOOK, *YOU COULD LOOK IT UP: THE LIFE OF CASEY STENGEL*

POP QUIZ

1. Who is the only player to be named World Series MVP twice—with two different teams?

....

2. After the All-Star Game was created in 1933, which Yankee was the first rookie to start in the midsummer classic?

....

3. Which Yankee catcher wore No. 32 before Elston Howard arrived in 1955?

....

4. Which Hall of Famer was Robinson Cano named after?

5. Who was the only manager to win world championships in his first two years?

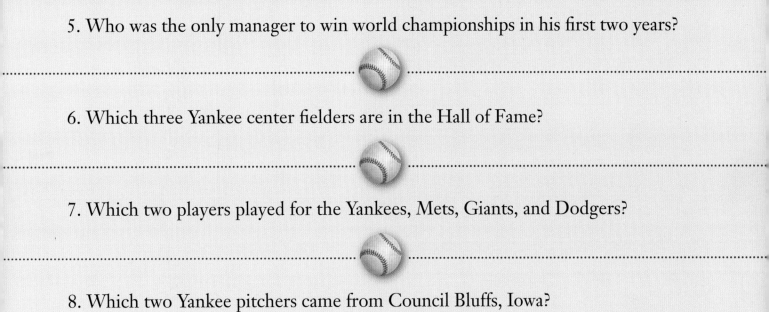

6. Which three Yankee center fielders are in the Hall of Fame?

7. Which two players played for the Yankees, Mets, Giants, and Dodgers?

8. Which two Yankee pitchers came from Council Bluffs, Iowa?

1: Reggie Jackson, with Oakland (1973) and New York (1977); 2: Joe DiMaggio, 1936; 3: Ralph Houk; 4: Jackie Robinson; 5: Ralph Houk; 6: Joe DiMaggio, Mickey Mantle, and Earle Combs; 7: Darryl Strawberry and Jose Vizcaino; 8: Stan Bahnsen and Jon Lieber

TO DROP A THIEF

Before he became a brash manager, Leo Durocher was a brash Yankee infielder on the 1928 championship team. He despised his famous roommate Babe Ruth, whom he called "that baboon." In return, Babe ridiculed the light-hitting Durocher, calling him "the All-American out."

Once, Ruth accused Durocher—who loved the nightlife and continually ran up debts—of stealing his wristwatch, which Durocher vehemently denied. "If I was going to steal anything from that big bum," he said angrily, "I'd steal his [expletive] Packard."

After the 1929 season, Durocher asked the Yankees for a raise to pay a large hotel bill. When General Manager Ed Barrow refused, Durocher cursed him. The next day he was sold to the Cincinnati Reds.

In 2002 spring training, a theft by a Yankee teammate again made headlines. Outfielder Ruben Rivera, who was making $1 million a year, took a glove from Derek Jeter's locker and sold it to a memorabilia dealer for $2,500. It was an unpardonable sin, even after Rivera returned the glove and apologized. The players convened and voted him off Yankee Island. Rivera was cut.

Leo Durocher

Ruben Rivera

Best Yankee Shortstops

MARK KOENIG (1925–1930)
This solid performer was on the Murderers'
Row teams.

FRANK CROSETTI (1932–1948)
Rizzuto's predecessor wore pinstripes for
37 consecutive years, as player and coach.

PHIL RIZZUTO (1941–1942, 1946–1956)
This beloved, undersized Hall of Famer was
the infield glue of championship teams.

TONY KUBEK (1957–1965)
A Rookie of the Year oft-remembered for being hit in the throat in the 1960 World Series.

DEREK JETER (1995–present)
He is the Joe DiMaggio of his generation.

Derek Jeter

COOL-HEADED

This cap represents NEW YORK as a whole. People wear it who want something HOT, who want something FASHIONABLE. We happen to have been hot the last few years.

—DEREK JETER IN THE 2005 BOOK *BLEEDING PINSTRIPES: A SEASON WITH THE BLEACHER CREATURES AT YANKEE STADIUM*, BY FILIP BONDY

Actor Denzel Washington sports a fashionable Yankee cap.

THANKS, KID

How does a 12-year-old Jersey boy become an overnight celebrity? Just by reaching over the fence and deflect Derek Jeter's long drive into the stands for a game-tying home run in Game 1 of the 1996 playoffs against the Baltimore Orioles.

That's exactly what Jeffrey Maier did, and faster than you can say "spectator interference," the "Kid Who Saved the Yankees" began to appear on national talk shows. He even got a ceremonial key to New York City from Yankee superfan Mayor Rudy Giuliani.

"This is *Yankee Stadium,*
in the middle of New York City.
We're not going to change it to some
cookie-cutter ballpark like Shea Stadium,
in the middle of nowheresville."

—ARCHITECT PERRY GREEN WHO SUPERVISED THE TWO-YEAR RENOVATION OF THE
ORIGINAL YANKEE STADIUM, IN *THE NEW YORK TIMES*, SEPTEMBER 30, 1973.

PEDRO VS. POPEYE

The blood feud between the Yankees and the Red Sox got seriously crazy during the 2003 American League Championship Series. A bench-clearing brawl in Fenway Park produced two unlikely combatants—flighty Red Sox pitcher Pedro Martinez and beefy, 72-year-old Yankee bench coach Don Zimmer.

In a scene almost too bizarre to believe, Martinez flung the charging Zimmer to the ground. Zimmer later apologized for getting carried away. Red Sox manager Grady Little, who still couldn't believe what he'd seen, put it best when he said, "We've upgraded from a battle to a war."

Don Zimmer

ROCKET VS. PIAZZA

When the Yankees and Mets faced each other in the 2000 World Series, it was more dramatic than anything playing on Broadway. Adding to the theatrics was the matchup between two superstar players, Roger Clemens and Mike Piazza. Only three months earlier, Roger Clemens's fastball had connected with Mike Piazza's head.

The situation devolved into a theater of the absurd when the Mets' slugger broke his bat on Clemens's pitch. The Yankees' ace angrily tossed the jagged bat barrel toward Piazza, who then yelled at Clemens, "What's your problem?" To this day, he's still waiting for an answer.

BOUTON'S BYGONES

Jim Bouton was a righty pitcher who was called "Bulldog" for his fierce competitiveness. Today he is perhaps better known for his controversial writing.

Bouton's *Ball Four*, a diary of his 1969 season with the Seattle Pilots and Houston Astros, stunned the baseball world with its revealing tales of what ballplayers said, did, and thought. His former Yankee teammates didn't think much of Bouton afterward, and he was *persona non grata* to the Yankees for nearly 30 years. Finally, in 1998, all was forgiven and Bouton was invited to Old-Timers' Day.

CONTROVERSIAL BOOKS BY YANKEES

Balls (1984) by Graig Nettles

The Bronx Zoo (1979) by Sparky Lyle

Perfect I'm Not: Boomer on Beer, Brawls, Backaches, and Baseball (2003) by David Wells

Ball Four (1970) by Jim Bouton

"I'd never even read a book before this one."

—SPARKY LYLE ON THE PUBLICATION OF HIS BOOK, *THE BRONX ZOO*, IN THE MAY 13, 1979, *THE NEW YORK TIMES*

RYNE'S REDEMPTION

Ryne Duren was the Yankees' hard-throwing, hard-drinking reliever with Coke-bottle glasses. He occasionally lost control. And he certainly lost it during the 1958 pennant-clinching party when he brawled with coach Ralph Houk. Now a recovering alcoholic, Duren later apologized to Houk, admitting that he'd had too much to drink.

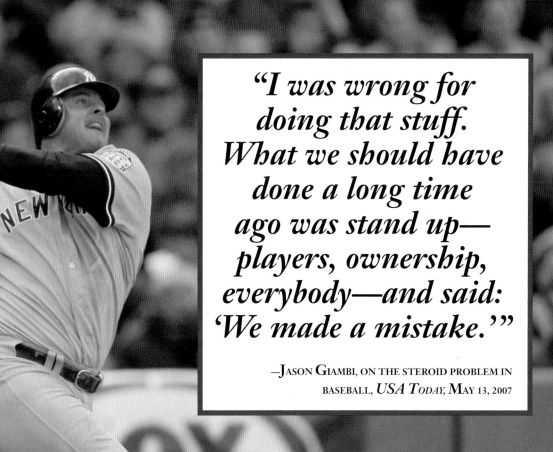

"*I was wrong for doing that stuff. What we should have done a long time ago was stand up— players, ownership, everybody—and said: 'We made a mistake.'*"

—Jason Giambi, on the steroid problem in baseball, *USA Today*, May 13, 2007

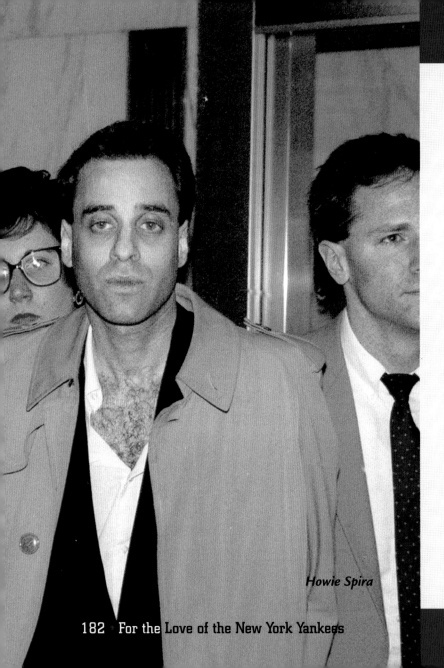

Howie Spira

STUPID OWNER TRICKS

George Steinbrenner got booted out of baseball in 1990 for consorting with a small-time mobster to dig up dirt on Dave Winfield, one of his own players. It certainly wasn't the proudest moment of the Boss's ownership of the Yankees. Steinbrenner paid $40,000 to Howie Spira to dig up detrimental information on his star outfielder, with whom he'd been feuding. At the time of his "life ban," *Newsweek* described Steinbrenner as the "Most Hated Man in Baseball."

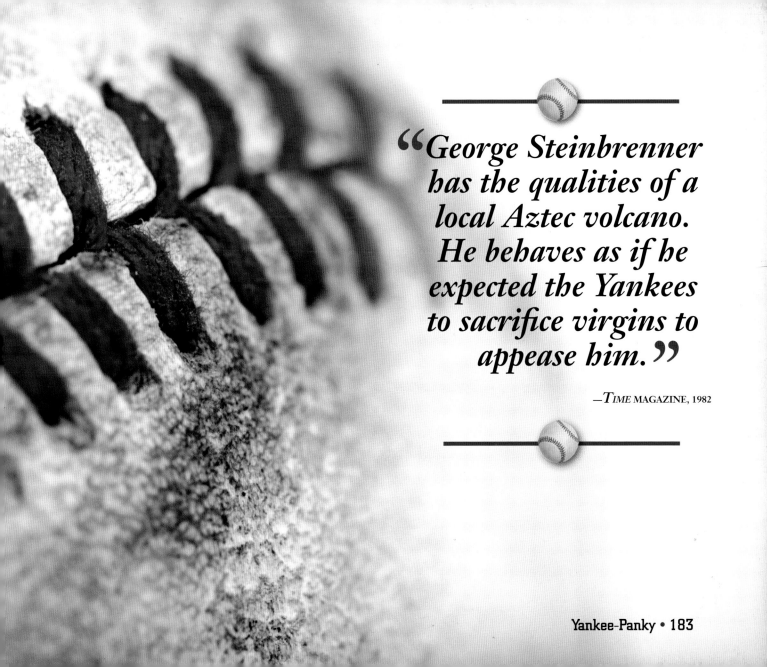

> **"George Steinbrenner has the qualities of a local Aztec volcano. He behaves as if he expected the Yankees to sacrifice virgins to appease him."**
>
> —*TIME* MAGAZINE, 1982

HERE'S CASEY

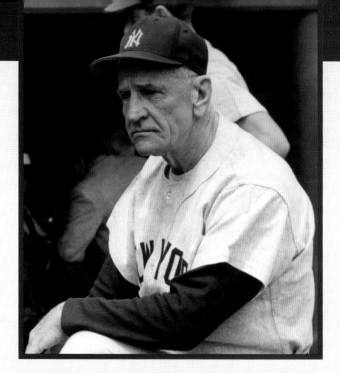

When the Yankees called a press conference after the 1948 season to introduce their new manager, Casey Stengel, the reaction was one of disbelief. They were kidding, right? Did they really just hire a clownish 58-year-old nonentity who had been out of the majors for five years? Why would they hire the leader of sad-sack Boston and Brooklyn teams in the 1930s and '40s?

It was no joke. Coming off a third-place finish in 1948, the Yankees would now be run by a man best-known as a prankster when he was a player and a loser as a manager. "The Yankees," wrote Boston sportswriter Dave Egan, "have now been mathematically eliminated from the 1949 pennant race." However, George Weiss, the new general manager, had known Stengel for years. Weiss knew he was unorthodox, but he also knew Stengel had never had the horses to win. Stengel was also a terrific tutor of young players. Soon, Weiss knew he had made one of his best decisions.

The Ol' Perfessor, as he was known, was a teacher who drew on his 40 years of experience in the game to show his players how to make the most of their physical and mental skills. The result was astounding. In Stengel's first five seasons, the Yankees won an unprecedented five straight championships. The wise-cracking, acerbic Stengel would helm 12 seasons in the Bronx, winning 10 pennants and 7 World Series. He also got one last laugh, earning a plaque in Cooperstown in 1966.

STAT LINE

Casey Stengel's Managerial Career

Team	Years	W–L	Pennants	World Championships
Dodgers	1934–36	208–251	0	0
Braves	1938–43	373–491	0	0
Yankees	1949–60	1,149–696	10	7
Mets	1962–65	175–404	0	0
Total	25 years	1,905–1,842	10	7

"The secret of managing a club is to keep the five guys who hate you away from the five who are undecided."

—CASEY STENGEL

NASTY IN '90

How bad were the 1990 Yankees? Well, Andy Hawkins pitched a no-hitter against the White Sox and still lost, thanks to three eighth-inning errors. The Yankees finished the season 67–95, in last place for the first time in 24 years.

"*Hating the New York Yankees is as American as apple pie, unwed mothers, and cheating on your income tax.*"

—MIKE ROYKO IN THE *CHICAGO SUN-TIMES* IN 1981

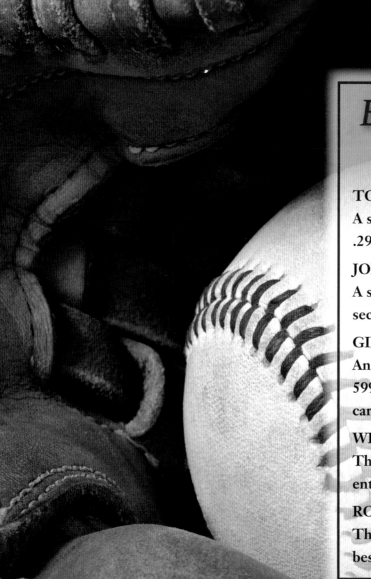

Best Yankee Second Basemen

TONY LAZZERI (1926–1937)
A smart, clutch-hitting Hall of Famer, he had a .292 career average.

JOE GORDON (1938–1943, 1946)
A superb all-around player, his 246 homers as a second baseman are an AL record.

GIL McDOUGALD (1951–1960)
An amazingly versatile infielder who played 599 games at second in an underrated 10-year career.

WILLIE RANDOLPH (1976–1988)
This six-time All-Star had to adjust to 31 different Yankee shortstops.

ROBINSON CANO (2005–present)
This silky .300 hitter could be the Yankees' best ever.

A BEAUTIFUL SAVE

Second baseman Billy Martin was a
skinny kid with big ears and a beak
nose. But he looked beautiful during
his running, shoestring catch of Jackie
Robinson's pop fly with two on base.
His glorious catch ended the seventh
inning of Game 7 and helped secure
the 1952 World Series for the Yankees.

COOKED GOOSE

Goose Gossage was in his prime in 1979, and the Yankees were favored to win a third consecutive champion- ship. That is, until April 19, when Goose got into a calamitous shower fight with a teammate. Big Cliff Johnson fell on Goose's right hand, which then required thumb sur- gery. With that injury, Yankee title hopes evaporated.

THE GREAT GOOFY

As great as Lefty Gomez was—he won 189 games pitching for the Yankees from 1930 to 1942—he was as goofy as anyone who ever put on pinstripes.

He always cracked on his teammates, and he joined vaudeville following the 1932 World Series. When his playing career ended, he instructed another fun-loving pitcher named Eddie Ford and gave him the nickname "Whitey." Later, Gomez joined the sales department of a sporting goods store. A question on the employment form asked why he had left his last job. Gomez wrote, "I couldn't get anybody out."

FOWL PLAY

While playing center field on August 4, 1983, in Toronto's Exhibition Stadium, Dave Winfield threw a baseball to try and scare a seagull off the field. Unfortunately, his warning toss bounced off the artificial turf and killed the bird.

Was it intentional? After the game, Toronto police said it was criminal and booked Winfield on a charge of cruelty to animals. Fortunately for Winfield, the charges were dropped.

SCOOTER PERSPECTIVE

"Well, that kind of puts a damper on even a Yankee win."

—Phil Rizzuto wrapping up the August 6, 1978,
broadcast by noting the death of Pope Paul VI

CHAPTER FIVE

YOU MUST REMEMBER THIS

"Playing 18 years in
Yankee Stadium
for you folks was the best thing that could ever happen to a ballplayer. "

—MICKEY MANTLE TO A CROWD OF 60,096 AS HIS NO. 7 WAS RETIRED ON JUNE 8, 1969

AN IMPERFECT PITCHER'S PERFECT GAME

Tension crackled throughout Yankee Stadium on October 8, 1956. The 64,519 souls in attendance were mesmerized by the unfolding history. Pitcher Don Larsen, who, a few days earlier, had been bombed by the Brooklyn Dodgers in Game 2 of the World Series, was in perfect control, flirting with immortality.

With three outs to go, Larsen's control began to slip. "I'm not what you call a real praying man," he said later, "but in the ninth inning I said to myself, 'Help me out somebody.'"

Somehow, Larsen withstood the unbearable pressure. On his 97th pitch, he struck out Dale Mitchell,

Berra and Larsen celebrate.

an excellent contact hitter, for the final out of the only perfect game in World Series history. The fans erupted in the stadium, catcher Yogi Berra bear-hugged Larsen, and the Yankees poured out of the dugout in a bellowing mass.

More than a half-century later, the idea of Don Larsen pitching a perfect game in the Fall Classic still seems perfectly implausible. Here's why:

- Two seasons prior to his perfect game, his record was 3–21, and he finished his career 81–91.
- He adopted a no-windup delivery only two weeks before the World Series.
- He had just blown a 6–0 lead in Game 2 of the World Series.

Hank Bauer

THE GOLDEN DOZEN

These 12 players were on the Yankee roster for five consecutive world championships (1949–1953):

Hank Bauer

Yogi Berra

Jerry Coleman

Joe Collins

Ralph Houk

Eddie Lopat

Johnny Mize

Vic Raschi

Allie Reynolds

Phil Rizzuto

Charlie Silvera

Gene Woodling

AN OSCAR PERFORMANCE

With his tumbleweed-size Afro, Oscar Gamble wasn't your typical-looking Yankee. Nor was he exactly a Yankee historian, as *Cleveland Press* reporter Bob Sudyk learned during a 1976 interview.

> Sudyk: "Who was the Sultan of Swat?"
>
> Gamble: "The what?"
>
> Sudyk: "Who was the Iron Horse?"
>
> Gamble: [shrugs]
>
> Sudyk: "OK, who was the Yankee Clipper?"
>
> Gamble: "George Steinbrenner. He made me cut my Afro."

Gamble before his meeting with the "Yankee Clipper"

THE STREAK

Part of the Yankee's 1941 season became more than national conversation—it was a national obsession. While Americans were concerned with conflict overseas, they were also spellbound by Joe DiMaggio's hitting streak. In every bar, living room, or anywhere with a radio tuned to baseball, DiMaggio was the big news. Did he get a hit? How long can he keep it up? He was the topic *du jour* in every ballpark, where the scoreboards tracked his feat.

The streak began on May 15, when he singled off Chicago's Edgar Smith before only 9,040 fans at Yankee Stadium.

Soon enough, DiMaggio's unstoppable hitting commanded daily attention from sports fans across the country.

As summer approached, DiMaggio continued his hitting assault, topping the record set by Wee Willie Keeler, who had hit safely in 44 consecutive games in 1897. On and on he went, providing "the most consistent performance under pressure I've ever seen," according to teammate Bill Dickey.

Three hits in Cleveland brought his amazing streak to 56 games, but there it ended. The next day, on July 17, before 67,468 fans, DiMaggio was robbed of hits twice by the Indians' third baseman. Only discouraged for an instant, DiMaggio began a 16-game hitting streak the next day.

Tony Kubek

SPEECHLESS

In the 1960 World Series, Bill Virdon's routine double-play grounder struck Yankee shortstop Tony Kubek in the throat, setting up the Pirates' five-run eighth inning in Game 7. Kubek could barely talk and was removed from the game, suffering from a bruised larynx. Fortunately, the incident had no effect on his later career in broadcasting.

BEST YANKEE RIGHT-HANDERS

Waite Hoyt (1921–1930) Hoyt won 157 games in his 10 years with the Yankees.

Red Ruffing (1930–1942, 1945–1946) A Hall of Famer and 273-game-winner, he drove in more runs than any pitcher in major-league history.

Vic Raschi (1946–1953) The Springfield Rifle threw bullets and assembled three straight 21-win seasons.

Allie Reynolds (1947–1954) Superchief was a double-duty mainstay of the Yankee dynasty. He won seven and saved four World Series games.

Mel Stottlemyre (1964–1974) This classy ace of some not-so-great Yankee teams still managed to win 20 or more games in three seasons.

Catfish Hunter (1975–1979) He contributed mightily to the 1976–1978 pennants.

A-ROD IN THE APPLE

The February 16, 2004, trade that brought Alex Rodriguez from the Texas Rangers to the New York Yankees wasn't just a blockbuster—it was off the charts. For starters, it involved a huge amount of money, and Texas agreed to pay $67 million of the $179 million remaining on A-Rod's record 10-year, $252 million contract.

At 28, A-Rod was the biggest star in the baseball galaxy. He was the reigning MVP and one of only three players (including Babe Ruth and Jimmie Foxx) to get at least 35 home runs, 100 runs, and 100 RBI in seven consecutive seasons. Yankee owner George Steinbrenner likened acquiring Rodriguez to bringing Reggie Jackson to New York nearly 30 years earlier.

A great shortstop, A-Rod voluntarily moved to third base in deference to Derek Jeter. And while he had been traded for a rising young talent (second baseman Alfonso Soriano), the consensus was that the Yankees had pulled off an old-fashioned heist.

> *"Derek [Jeter], being the leader of the team, he does it with elegance and class and grace. I'm here to assist him, be ONE of THE GUYS."*
>
> —ALEX RODRIGUEZ AT HIS
> 2004 INTRODUCTORY PRESS CONFERENCE
> AS A YANKEE

David Cone celebrates his perfect game with his teammates.

THE PERFECT DAY

July 18, 1999, was a scorcher at Yankee Stadium. On the field, special guests fanned themselves during the ceremony for Yogi Berra Day, which saw the legendary Yankee backstop catch the ceremonial first pitch from his famous perfect game battery mate, Don Larsen.

In a short time, everyone would be sweating through one of the most dramatic moments in Yankee history. Pitcher David Cone cruised through the Montreal Expos' lineup inning after inning, giving up neither hit nor walk. He pitched a perfect game. Déjà vu all over again, indeed.

I want to THANK EVERYONE for making this night necessary.

—YOGI BERRA ON AUGUST 26, 1947, WHEN FANS FROM HIS HOMETOWN OF ST. LOUIS HELD A DAY FOR HIM AT SPORTSMAN'S PARK

FROM CY YOUNG TO SAYONARA

To many observers, Sparky Lyle's trade from the Red Sox to the Yankees in 1972 was an updated version of the infamous Babe Ruth deal. It put added pox on the Sox and sparked the Yankees to glory.

In 1977—the Yankees' first world championship in 15 years—Lyle became the first American League reliever to win the Cy Young Award. Yet, a month later the Yankees signed Goose Gossage, preferring his 100-mile-per-hour fastball to Lyle's 80-mile-per-hour slider. In 1979, Lyle was traded to the Texas Rangers.

Sparky Lyle

CY YOUNG YANKEES

The Cy Young Award, which goes to each league's best pitcher, was created in 1956 in honor of the 511-game-winning Hall of Famer. Before 1967, only one award was given for both leagues. Yankee winners are:

YEAR	PITCHER	W–L	ERA
1958	Bob Turley	21–7	2.97
1961	Whitey Ford	25–4	3.21
1977	Sparky Lyle	13–5 (26 Saves)	2.17
1978	Ron Guidry	25–3	1.74
2001	Roger Clemens	20–3	3.51

NONE BETTER THAN MO

There's the splitter and the sinker, but there's no pitch like Mariano Rivera's cutter. This nearly unhittable pitch made Rivera one of the greatest closers in baseball history. Amazingly, it's a pitch he stumbled upon by accident.

In 1997, two years after he joined the Yankees, Rivera was playing catch with teammate Ramiro Mendoza. His throws kept sliding to the left. Mendoza was surprised by the movement and urged Rivera to try throwing it the same way in the game. Rivera's cutter—a 95-mile-per-hour "cut" fastball—became the top knockout pitch for the bullpen champion.

BEST YANKEE RELIEF PITCHERS

Mariano Rivera (1995–present) He's as close to automatic as there's ever been. Nobody's calmer or better.

Goose Gossage (1978–1983, 1989) An intimidating fireballer, he frequently pitched two or three innings to close games.

Sparky Lyle (1972–1978) A great practical joker who put the Yankee bullpen on the map in the 1970s.

Dave Righetti (1979, 1981–1990) Acquired from Texas for Sparky Lyle, he made a smooth transition from starter to closer with 224 career saves as a Yankee.

Johnny Murphy (1932–1943, 1946) The foremost relief specialist of his era, he led the league in saves four times.

Mariano Rivera figure

THE IRON IDOL

On June 1, 1925, manager Miller Huggins sent up a strapping 21-year-old rookie from Columbia University named Lou Gehrig to pinch-hit for shortstop Pee Wee Wanninger in the eighth inning against Washington, then Huggins inserted him at first base to replace Wally Pipp. The next day, Pipp was hit in the head in batting practice and complained of a headache. Huggins turned to the young Gehrig and said, "You're my first baseman today and from now on." Gehrig was the son of German immigrant parents and grew up on the streets of New York City. He remains the greatest ballplayer the city ever produced.

Thus began the legend of the Iron Horse, the greatest first baseman of all time, the most durable, inspirational, and tragic player ever to wear pinstripes—the Pride of the Yankees. During his 17-year, all-Yankee career, he batted .340 and played in an astounding 2,130 consecutive games, a testament to his unparalleled toughness. He fractured bones in his fingers on 17 separate occasions, suffered a concussion after a beaning, but on he played. And how he played!

Teamed with Babe Ruth, Gehrig became half of the most murderous one-two tandem in baseball history. Gehrig batted in 140 or more runs in eight different seasons, hit 493 career homers, and won the Triple Crown in 1934 with a .363 average, 49 homers, and 165 RBI. By the time he retired, he had set 25 major-league records—including 23 grand slams. Also, in a 1932 game against Philadelphia, he became the first player in the 20th century to hit four home runs in one game.

Yet for most of his career, Gehrig played in the abundant shadow of Ruth and his outsized personality. That was just fine for the humble, painfully shy star. When Ruth was gone by the mid-1930s, Gehrig was again obscured. Although Lou exploded for a .354 average with 49 homers in 1936—sparking the first of four consecutive Yankee world championships—

the press and fans were more fascinated by rookie sensation Joe DiMaggio.

Still, that didn't matter to Gehrig. He was the captain, the leader by example, and the ultimate team man. "I'm not a headline guy, and we might as well face it," Gehrig said. "I'm just a guy who's in there every day."

Gehrig played in every Yankee game from June 1925 to 1938, but in spring training in 1939, he felt that something was terribly wrong. His strength, stamina, and reflexes were gone. In May, without complaint or self-pity, he benched himself. At 35, Gehrig had been stricken by a mysterious disease, which is now known as amyotrophic lateral sclerosis (ALS) or Lou Gehrig's disease.

On July 4, 1939, on Lou Gehrig Appreciation Day, the once-indestructible soul was the center of attention. Amid farewell gifts and speeches, he appeared too weak to stand, too emotional to speak. Then he wiped his eyes, got himself under control, and told his teammates, old and new, as well as 62,000 fans, he was the "luckiest man on the face of the earth." Less than two years later, he was gone.

Gehrig and Ruth

MOST EVER, BEST EVER?

Were the 1998 champion Yankees the greatest team ever? Well, nobody resembled Ruth or Reggie and aside from pitcher David Wells, they didn't have any starters in the All-Star Game. But they did have a great team spirit and won 114 regular-season games. Also, they had the best winning percentage (.704) since the famed 1927 Murderers' Row team. And they won 11 games in three rounds of playoffs for a grand total of 125 victories—the most ever. But were they the best ever? Manager Joe Torre wouldn't say, except to note that his team was "a great *team* team."

EASYGOING JOE

People scoffed when 56-year-old Joe Torre was named Yankee skipper in 1996. As manager of the Braves, Mets, and Cardinals, he'd never won a championship. Nor was he fiery or dynamic in the Steinbrenner style. The scoffing didn't last long, though, as Torre calmly guided the Yankees to four championships in his first five seasons.

Steinbrenner and Torre

THE FLIP

"What was Derek Jeter doing there?" some people asked in amazement. Those who knew Jeter weren't as amazed, since they knew that he was always in a position to win. The flip—Jeter's ultimate right place, right time moment—occurred during Game 3 of the 2001 American League Division Series in Oakland and has become baseball legend.

With the Yankees nursing a 1–0 lead in the seventh inning, the A's Terrence Long doubled to right and Jeremy Giambi tried to score from first base. When Yankee right fielder Shane Spencer overthrew two cutoff men, it looked like the A's would tie the game. Suddenly, Jeter swooped in, raced behind first base, and read the errant throw like a human GPS. He snared the ball on the run in foul territory and shoveled a 20-foot backhand flip to catcher Jorge Posada, who tagged Giambi out.

It was the heads-up play of a lifetime. The Yankees held their lead and won 1–0. They beat the A's in the series, and the flip became a signature achievement for Jeter.

Posada makes the tag on Jeremy Giambi following Jeter's (in foreground) flip.

Derek Jeter managed to get a ball from behind the first base line and flipped it, backhanded, to catcher Jorge Posada to make an out at home—all while the force of his body moved him away from his intended target. Those who saw Jeter's flip witnessed one of the most spectacular plays in Yankee history.

HEY, ABBOTT!

Born without a right hand, Jim Abbott was a profile of courage and perseverance during his 10-year major-league career. Never was he more inspirational than on September 4, 1993, when he threw a no-hitter and beat the Cleveland Indians, 4–0, at Yankee Stadium.

"I'll be the first to admit it. My knees were knocking in the ninth inning."

—Jim Abbott, recalling his no-hitter in *Baseball Digest*, May 2007

David Wells on his teammates' shoulders after his perfect game

YANKEE PERFECT GAMES

July 18, 1999
David Cone beat Montreal (6–0)

May 17, 1998
David Wells beat Minnesota (4–0)

October 8, 1956
Don Larsen beat Brooklyn (2–0)*

*World Series

YANKEES ABC's

R Reg-gie, Reg-gie

Reginald Martinez Jackson was the straw that stirred the drink in the 1970s. He battled with his manager, irritated his teammates, yet he still belted three home runs on three consecutive pitches in the 1977 World Series. He brought the Yankees their first championship in 15 years and staked his claim as Mr. October.

S Steinbrenner

This bombastic fellow from Cleveland is the most famous owner in sports. George Michael Steinbrenner purchased the Yankees for $10 million in 1973 and often acted like a schoolyard bully with his employees. Yet he could

Reggie Jackson

also be remarkably kind and generous and was never outspent in his pursuit of success. Now GMS has turned control of the club to sons Hank and Hal, who seem to have the same hard-driving DNA.

T Twenty-seven Up, Twenty-seven Down

The perfect game is not something the Yankees invented, but they find perfection like nobody else. Don Larsen's perfect game in the 1956 World Series remains one of the game's all-time classic moments. David Wells pitched a perfect game on Beanie Baby Day in 1998, followed by David Cone's perfect game on Yogi Berra Day in 1999. What other teams include perfection in their promotions?

U Utz

Utz is the official potato chip and pretzel of Yankee Stadium. A giant billboard featuring the Utz girl is located behind the right-field stands where the Bleacher Creatures sit and think peculiar thoughts. Some Creatures expressed concern that the Yankees, seeking a corporate naming opportunity, might rename the ballpark Utz Stadium.

David Wells

V Victory

It's something the Yankees are sort of familiar with. They have had a long tradition of victory since their very first on April 23, 1903, when they beat Washington, 7–2.

LIGHTNING STRIKES

At 5'11" and only 160 pounds, Ron Guidry was a small wonder. On June 17, 1978, during his second full season, the wiry lefty from Louisiana managed to start a Yankee tradition.

Armed with an explosive slider and a 95-mile-per-hour heater, Guidry struck out 18 California Angels and set both a franchise and American League record. It was a virtuoso performance that caused Yankee broadcaster Phil Rizzuto to keep excitedly calling Guidry, "Louisiana Lightning." Guidry even impressed strikeout king Nolan Ryan. "The kid was overpowering," said Ryan, who watched from the Angels' dugout.

Throughout the game, Yankee fans stood up, cheered, and clapped every time Guidry had two strikes. "When they start hollering and screaming, you just get pumped that much more," said Guidry, who called the 18-strikeout feat his single greatest thrill. Thanks to Guidry, the two-strike chanting and cheering became a Yankee Stadium tradition.

As it turned out, 1978 was a season of dominance for Guidry. He finished with a 25–3 record, a 1.74 ERA, and the Cy Young Award.

BEST YANKEE LEFT-HANDERS

Lefty Gomez (1930–1942) This Hall of Famer was fast with a quip and a pitch.

Eddie Lopat (1948–1955) "The Junk Man" was a fixture on five consecutive championship teams and later mentored Whitey Ford.

Whitey Ford (1950, 1953–1967) He was the toughest Yankee pitcher to beat, as proven by his impressive .690 winning percentage.

Ron Guidry (1975–1988) A three-time 20-game winner, he had only a two-pitch repertoire.

Andy Pettitte (1995–2003, 2007–present) This ace was a mainstay on six pennant-winners and four championship teams.

THE TURLEY SHOW

Trailing three games to one in the 1958 World Series against the Milwaukee Braves, the Yankees needed to be rescued. Enter "Bullet" Bob Turley, the '58 Cy Young Award winner. He won two of the last three games and saved the other, helping the Yankees win the series.

"Being on the mound for the final out in the World Series was the most exciting moment of my career."

—Bob Turley in *We Played the Game*

MUNSON CATCHING ON

It's not how you start; it's how you finish, right? Catcher Thurman Munson began his rookie year with one hit in 30 at-bats—but he ended the season batting .302. Munson also threw out 33 of 64 would-be base stealers and won 1970 Rookie of the Year honors.

WELL DONE, DONNIE!

Don Mattingly went on one of his patented tears in 1987. On July 18, he belted a home run off Texas's Jose Guzman for his eighth homer in eight consecutive games, tying a record set by Pittsburgh's Dale Long in 1956.

Donnie Baseball also hit a major-league-record six grand slams that season (a mark tied by Cleveland's Travis Hafner in 2006). Strangely enough, although Mattingly played for 14 years, he had never hit a grand slam before the 1987 season and never hit one after.

Don Mattingly and Lou Piniella

WHO'S MY MANAGER?

In his 14-year Yankee career, Don Mattingly played for his share of managers:

Buck Showalter 4 years (1992–1995)

Stump Merrill 1+ years (1990–1991)

Bucky Dent 1+ years (1989–1990)

Dallas Green 1 year (1989)

Lou Piniella 3 years (1986–1988)

Billy Martin 3 years (1983, 1985, 1988)

Yogi Berra 1+ years (1984–1985)

Clyde King 7 games (1982)

BOONE TO BUST

Aaron Boone's career with the Yankees lasted only three months, but his place in pinstripe history is secure. On October 16, 2003, the struggling third baseman blasted a home run off a Tim Wakefield knuckleball in the 11th inning of Game 7 of the ALCS. His hit gave the Yankees a 6–5 victory over the Red Sox and their 39th pennant.

After the season, the playoff hero hurt his knee playing pickup basketball. So, the Yankees went out and found a replacement—a guy named Alex Rodriguez.

I told him MAGICAL things happen here in the stadium. And I told him GHOSTS come out in October.

—DEREK JETER ON HIS PEP TALK TO AARON BOONE,
BOSTON GLOBE, OCTOBER 17, 2003

QUITE FINE IN '39

1939 was the year of *Gone With the Wind*, *The Wizard of Oz*, Lou Gehrig's farewell, and Ted Williams' debut. It was also the year the Yankees won their fourth consecutive championship. In his book *Baseball Dynasties: The Greatest Teams of All Time*, author Rob Neyer calls the 1939 Yankees the greatest team ever.

Bill Dickey was an important part of the '39 Yankees.

FINISHING SCHOOL

Here's a list of the Yankees' top minor-league affiliates through the years:

Scranton/Wilkes-Barre Yankees (2007–present)

Columbus Clippers (1979–2006)

Tacoma Yankees (1978)

Syracuse Chiefs (1967–1977)

Toledo Mud Hens (1965–1966)

Richmond Virginians (1956–1964)

Denver Bears (1955–1958)

Kansas City Blues (1937–1954)

Newark Bears (1931–1949)

Oakland Oaks (1935–1936)

Jersey City Skeeters (1930)

Chambersburg Young Yanks (1929)

Jersey City Colts (1922)

"*I can't say that I'm glad it's over. Of course I wanted to go on as long as I could. Now… I just want to get out there and keep helping to win ballgames.*"

—JOE DIMAGGIO AFTER THE END OF HIS 56-GAME HITTING STREAK, *NEW YORK DAILY NEWS,* JULY 18, 1941

COMEBACK KIDS

As every Yankee fan would love to forget, their heroes were on the wrong end of the biggest comeback in history when the Red Sox miraculously rallied from a three game deficit to win the 2004 ALCS. Yet, the Yankees are no strangers to impressive comebacks themselves.

- 2006: Trailing Texas 9–0 on May 16, the Yankees battled back and won 14–13 on Jorge Posada's two-run homer in the ninth.

- 2001: One out away from losing both Games 4 and 5 in the 2001 World Series against Arizona, the Yankees wound up winning both games in extra innings.

- 1996: Trailing Atlanta 6–0 in Game 4 of the World Series, the Yankees went on to win in the 10th inning, aided by Jim Leyritz's game-tying home run in the eighth.

- 1978: Trailing first-place Boston by 14 games on July 19, the Yankees evened the race and forced a one-game playoff to decide the AL pennant, which the Yankees won, thanks to a Bucky Dent home run.

- 1958: Trailing Milwaukee three games to one in the World Series, the Yankees became the first team since the 1925 Pirates to come back from such a deficit to win the World Series.

- 1950: Trailing Boston 9–0 in the sixth inning on April 18, the Yankees scored nine runs in the eighth and eventually won 15–10.

Fans at the 2001 World Series

Yankees celebrate their win in
Game 5 of the 2001 World Series.

Chris Chambliss attempts to round the bases.

SPIRIT OF '76

By 1976, what was once the greatest dynasty in sports had fallen and the team had gone 12 years without a championship. At the same time, the Yankees were forced from their own hallowed grounds—they shared Shea Stadium with the Mets for the 1974 and 1975 seasons while Yankee Stadium was refurbished. Yet, in 1976, the Yankees celebrated their homecoming and a return to glory with one fabled swing.

Facing the Kansas City Royals in a best-of-five ALCS (it wasn't expanded to a best-of-seven until 1985), it all came down to a nerve-wracking Game 5 finale. The score was tied 6–6 in the ninth inning when Chris Chambliss came up to bat against the Royals' Mark Littell. On a first-pitch fastball, Chambliss became a hero for the ages.

His blast over the fence in right-center won the Yankees their first pennant since 1964 and made long-suffering fans ecstatic.

As Chambliss circled the bases, he was swarmed by a mob from the stands. "I was worried about getting trampled," he said. Chambliss never even touched home plate, as a fan had already taken it.

Chambliss celebrates his homer.

BERNIE TRIFECTA

Bernie Williams, the guitar-playing center fielder, had a platinum year during the Yankees' remarkable 114-win season in 1998. Williams hit .339 to win the batting title; he also won a Gold Glove and a World Series ring. He is the only player in history to win all three in one season.

YANKEE BATTING TITLES

1998 Bernie Williams (.339)

1994 Paul O'Neill (.359)

1984 Don Mattingly (.343)

1956 Mickey Mantle (.353)

1945 Snuffy Stirnweiss (.309)

1940 Joe DiMaggio (.352)

1939 Joe DiMaggio (.381)

1934 Lou Gehrig (.363)

1924 Babe Ruth (.378)

MANTLE MEASURES UP

On April 17, 1953, Washington lefty Chuck Stobbs threw a pitch that Mickey Mantle nearly rocketed into orbit. Yankee PR director Red Patterson raced out of Griffith Stadium and calculated that the ball had traveled 565 feet, giving birth to the term "tape-measure home run."

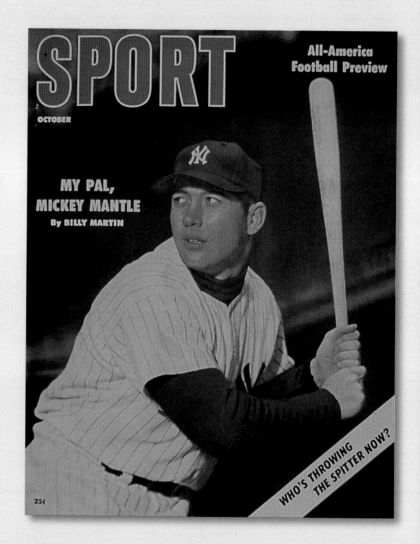

SPORT

OCTOBER

All-America Football Preview

MY PAL, MICKEY MANTLE
By BILLY MARTIN

WHO'S THROWING THE SPITTER NOW?

25¢

MANTLE BY THE NUMBERS

- 16-time All-Star (1952–1965, 1967–1968)
- Triple Crown winner (1956)
- 12 World Series appearances
- Most homers (18) and RBI (40) in World Series history
- Three-time AL MVP (1956, 1957, 1962)
- Most games played by a Yankee (2,401)

Born: 10/20/31

Died: 8/13/95

Hall of Fame Election: 1974

G	AB	H	R	HR	RBI	BA	SB
2,401	8,102	2,415	1,677	536	1,509	.298	153

CHAPTER SIX

ULTIMATE RIVALRY

"Lots of people look up to Billy Martin.
That's because he just knocked them down."

—JIM BOUTON

THE BEGINNING OF THE CURSE

No, Babe Ruth never actually put a hex on the Red Sox. Still, almost every misfortune that befell Babe's former team for more than eight decades was blamed on the world-famous Curse of the Bambino. Silly superstition or not, here's the Ruth truth: Boston owner Harry Frazee, in a financial bind, unloaded his star pitcher on December 26, 1919, to the Yankees for $125,000 and a $350,000 loan, beginning a long line of Sox blunders and bad luck.

At the time of the Ruth deal, the Red Sox had won four of the last eight World Series and the Yankees had yet to win a championship. Yet as a Yankee, Ruth revolutionized the game with the home run, became America's most idolized sports hero, and transformed his club into a model of power and success. Following the trade, the Sox would not win another championship for 84 years.

So, the curse became a coping mechanism for beleaguered Boston fans. How else could championship-starved Red Sox rooters explain their team's haunting failures? Why else would Johnny Pesky hesitate for a split second to allow the winning run to score in the 1946 World Series? Why else would Bill Buckner allow that grounder to go through his legs in the 1986 World Series?

In reality, the idea of a curse came to light in 1986 following the Red Sox loss to the Mets. As George Vecsey of *The New York Times* wrote, "All the ghosts and demons and curses of the past 68 years continued to haunt the Boston Red Sox." Then he cited Ruth and 1918, the Red Sox's last championship season: "Yet the owner sold him to the lowly New York Yankees to finance one of his Broadway shows, and for 68 years it has never been the same." The headline of the article read, "Babe Ruth Curse Strikes Again." A few years later, *Boston Globe* columnist Dan Shaughnessy wrote a best seller called *The*

Curse of the Bambino, detailing the doom and heartache of Red Sox Nation. The idea of this mystical phenomenon became popular, and whenever the Red Sox found a way to lose a big game, often under odd circumstances, many believed the curse was surely the cause.

Of course, it all ended in 2004 when the Red Sox made the greatest comeback in baseball history, rallying from a three-game deficit in the ALCS against the Yankees. They went on to sweep St. Louis in the World Series, ending generations of heartbreak. The curse had been broken.

But when it comes to the Red Sox–Yankees rivalry, it seems belief in superstitions, jinxes, and hexes never dies. Construction worker and Red Sox fan Gino Castignoli buried a David Ortiz jersey in the foundation of the new Yankee Stadium in 2008. However, the jinxed jersey was excavated and the curse-minded Red Sox fan was fired. The jersey later sold for $175,100 in a charity auction.

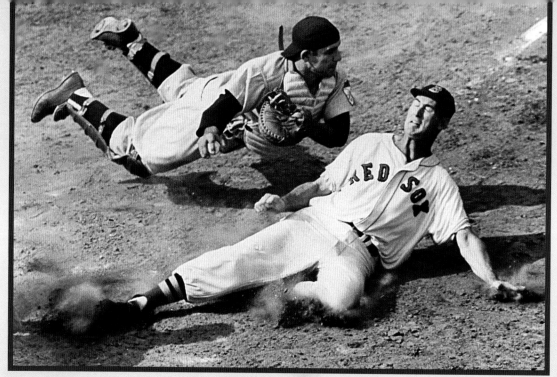

Berra and Williams

UNDONE DEAL

Ted Williams and Joe DiMaggio, the epicenter of the Red Sox–Yankees rivalry from 1939 to 1951, were the iconic faces of their respective franchises. Incredibly, Joltin' Joe and the Splendid Splinter were almost traded for each other. In April 1947, Red Sox owner Tom Yawkey and Yankee boss Dan Topping agreed over drinks to swap the two players. Then Yawkey, fearing a Fenway fan backlash, asked if the Yankees would throw in the raw rookie outfielder-catcher Yogi Berra. Wisely, the Yankees scotched the deal.

> **"It was very different the way Boston treated WILLIAMS and New York treated DIMAGGIO.... The New York temperament rallied around Joe. He was kind of classy and they liked that."**
>
> —JOHN UPDIKE IN *RED SOX NATION*, BY PETER GOLENBOCK

BOSTON MASSACRE

While no Red Sox fans jumped into the Charles River on September 10, 1978, there was still a whopping sense of fatalism in Boston following the Yankees' murderous four-game sweep in the now-famous Boston Massacre.

The Red Sox had a 14-game lead for the pennant on July 19, prompting Reggie Jackson to say, "Not even Alydar can catch them." But the Yankees scored 42 runs in the September sweep, and they left town tied for first.

Rick Burleson makes a tag on Willie Randolph in the 9/8/78 Yankees–Red Sox game.

MEDDLESOME NETTLES

"**THERE'S NO WAY TO BEAT HIM. We** could handcuff his right arm to his left leg and his left arm to his right leg, put a ball and chain around his neck and a blindfold around his eyes, and he would still make the play."

—Dodger Rick Monday on Graig Nettles, who had robbed Los Angeles of seven possible extra-base hits during the 1978 World Series, Sports Illustrated, October 23, 1978

WHAT WERE THEY THINKING?

The Yankees–Red Sox rivalry is the nastiest and oldest in American sports. In some ways, Yankee superiority through the years can be attributed to the Red Sox's spectacularly bad trades with the Yankees.

MARCH 22, 1972
The Red Sox trade reliever Sparky Lyle to the Yankees for Danny Cater and a player to be named later (Mario Guerrero). Lyle helped the Yankees win three consecutive pennants (1976–1978), and he won the Cy Young Award in 1977.

MAY 6, 1930
Red Ruffing, who was 39–96 with the Red Sox, is traded to the Yanks for Cedric Durst and $50,000. Ruffing proceeded to win 231 games for the Yankees (at least 20 per season from 1936 to 1939) and was part of six world championship teams.

Red Ruffing

JANUARY 30, 1923

The Red Sox trade lefty Herb Pennock for Camp Skinner, Norm McMillan, George Murray, and cash. Pennock averaged 19 wins for the Yankees from 1923 to 1928, collected three World Series rings, and was inducted into the Hall of Fame.

DECEMBER 15, 1920

The Red Sox trade Waite Hoyt, Harry Harper, Mike McNally, and Wally Schang for Muddy Ruel, Del Pratt, Sammy Vick, and Hank Thormahlen. Hoyt, as a Yankee, averaged 17 wins per season from 1921 to 1929 and was inducted into Cooperstown.

JANUARY 3, 1920

The Red Sox sell Babe Ruth to the Yankees for $125,000 and a $350,000 loan against the mortgage on Fenway Park. In 1923, Ruth led the team to its first world championship and was instrumental in the club building a new stadium, later nicknamed "The House That Ruth Built." Today, he is generally acknowledged as the greatest player in baseball history.

HERB PENNOCK

BIG LEAGUE CHEWING GUM

BILL VIRDON

Bill Virdon was the only Yankees manager in more than 80 years who never managed a game in Yankee Stadium. He ran the show at Shea Stadium through 1974 and most of 1975.

George Steinbrenner and Bill Virdon

❝_I have known Mr. Torre for a good majority of my adult life, and there has been no bigger influence on my professional development. His class, dignity, and the way he respected those around him—from ballplayers to batboys—are all qualities that are easy to admire, but difficult to duplicate._**❞**

—Derek Jeter on October 22, 2007, in his first public statement about Joe Torre's departure from the Yankees

RUTHLESS FEAT

There was a lot of hubbub when Roger Maris broke Babe Ruth's hallowed home run record on October 1, 1961. But a record Babe treasured even more was broken seven days later—and with little fanfare. That was when Whitey Ford—whose amazing 25–4 season was overshadowed by Maris's home run exploits—broke Ruth's consecutive scoreless inning streak in the World Series.

Ruth, a great athlete who began his career as a pitcher, was enormously proud that he had tossed 29⅔ consecutive shutout innings while leading the Red Sox to World Series championships in 1916 and 1918. He often said it was his most cherished feat. Ford was unaware that he was getting close to Babe's longstanding record. When he was told he had eclipsed it with his 14 scoreless frames in Games 1 and 4 of the '61 Series against Cincinnati, Ford quipped, "It sure has been a rough year for the Babe."

Ford eventually raised his World Series scoreless inning streak to 33⅔ innings against San Francisco in the '62 Fall Classic.

THE EVIL EMPIRE

The high stakes in the star wars between the Yankees and Red Sox were raised again on December 26, 2002. Enraged that the Yankees had beat out his team for Cuban defector Jose Contreras to the tune of $32 million, Red Sox president Larry Lucchino lashed out. Lucchino used the terminology President Reagan had used to refer to the Soviet Union in the early 1980s and so created an infamous Yankee nickname. "The evil empire," he said, "extends its tentacles even into Latin America."

Jose Contreras

"*That's B.S. That's how
a sick person thinks.
I've learned this about
Lucchino. He's baseball's
foremost* CHAMELEON
of all time. He CHANGES
COLORS DEPENDING
on where he's standing."

—GEORGE STEINBRENNER IN RESPONSE TO LUCCHINO'S "EVIL
EMPIRE" COMMENT, *BOSTON GLOBE*, DECEMBER 30, 2002

SHEA IT AIN'T SO

The Yankees made Shea Stadium their temporary home during the 1974 and 1975 seasons. But it wasn't where their hearts were. Forced to share the Mets' ballpark while Yankee Stadium underwent major renovations, the Yankees suffered a few indignities there. Star player Bobby Murcer went nearly the entire 1974 season homerless at Shea.

The next season, center fielder Elliott Maddox tore up his knee in the outfield, and then filed a lawsuit against the Yankees, the Mets, and Shea's maintenance company. By 1976, the Yankees were glad to say goodbye to Shea.

The Yankee Record at Shea Stadium

YEAR	WINS	LOSSES	AVG.	POSITION IN AL EAST
1974	89	73	.549	2nd
1975	83	77	.519	3rd

TALKIN' RIVALRY

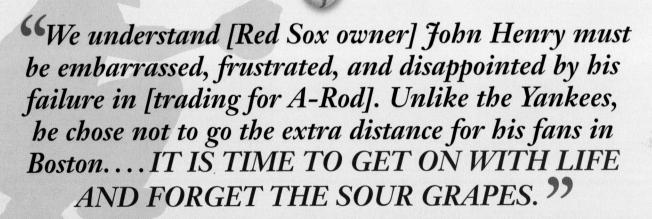

"*I know there are 650 or 700 other players who are sleeping this morning. Either that, or they're taking their kids to school. But there's no way they're going to be up running the stairs or DOING WHAT I'M DOING.*"

—ALEX RODRIGUEZ, *THE RECORD* (BERGEN COUNTY, NEW JERSEY), JANUARY 30, 2005

"*We understand [Red Sox owner] John Henry must be embarrassed, frustrated, and disappointed by his failure in [trading for A-Rod]. Unlike the Yankees, he chose not to go the extra distance for his fans in Boston....IT IS TIME TO GET ON WITH LIFE AND FORGET THE SOUR GRAPES.*"

—GEORGE STEINBRENNER, *ASSOCIATED PRESS*, FEBRUARY 18, 2004

"*A whole range of products has been created to reflect this toxicity. 'YANKEES SUCK' T-shirts and 'YANKEE HATER' hats and shirts are among the most tasteful products to be found throughout Red Sox Nation.*"

—ALAN M. KLEIN, *GROWING THE GAME: THE GLOBALIZATION OF MAJOR-LEAGUE BASEBALL*, 2006

"*THIS IS A YANKEE COUNTRY. We're going to put the Yankees back on top and restore the universe to order.*"

—HANK STEINBRENNER ON RED SOX NATION, *THE NEW YORK TIMES*, MARCH 2, 2008

"*This isn't just
a ballclub! This is
Murderers' Row!*"

—SPORTSWRITER ARTHUR ROBINSON IN 1927

PRIZE CATCH

Suffice it to say, Jim "Catfish" Hunter was one whale of a pitcher, winning 21 or more games every year between 1971 and 1975. Not surprisingly, the Yankees made the Oakland free agent the highest-paid player in history on New Year's Eve 1974, with a five-year, $3.5 million contract. Catfish's best years were with the A's, but he was still a great Yankee workhorse and easily the most popular player among his teammates. He appeared in three World Series in the Bronx before arm trouble and diabetes ended his career at age 33 in 1979. His plaque in Cooperstown reads, "The bigger the game, the better he pitched."

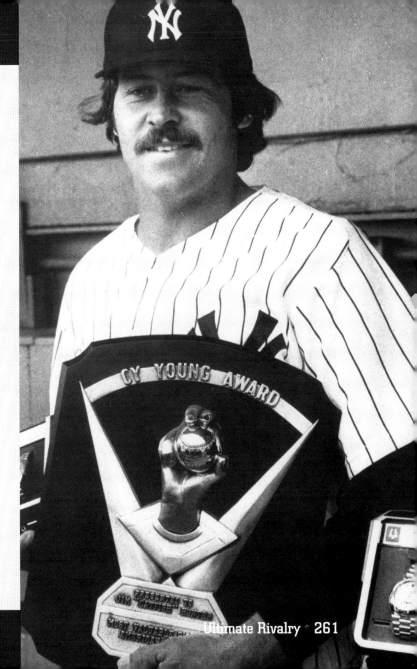

POP QUIZ

1. How many grand slams did Roger Maris hit during his record 61-home run campaign in 1961?

2. Which Yankee played a brain surgeon in an episode of the soap opera *General Hospital?*

3. Who was the first rookie pitcher to win an All-Star Game?

4. What percentage of Goose Gossage's 310 career saves resulted from two or more innings of relief?

5. Which player did the Yankees get when they traded Roger Maris to the Cardinals in 1966?

6. Which pitcher began his career with the Red Sox in 1967 and played for the Yankees from 1972 to 1978?

7. Who was the only player to collect an All-Star Game hit at Yankee Stadium, the Polo Grounds, and Ebbets Field?

8. Which Yankee wore uniform No. 21 before Paul O'Neill?

DAMN YANKEES

No team has enjoyed sheer domination as the Yankees have, winning consecutive championships from 1949 to 1953. In 1954, the Cleveland Indians, who had won an AL-record 111 games, foiled their attempt at a six-peat. This inspired the Douglas Wallop novel *The Year the Yankees Lost the Pennant*, which in turn inspired the legendary musical *Damn Yankees*. Starring Gwen Verdon as the vamp Lola and Tab Hunter as a Washington Senators fan who sells his soul to the devil, *Damn Yankees* debuted on Broadway in 1955 and ran for more than 1,000 performances.

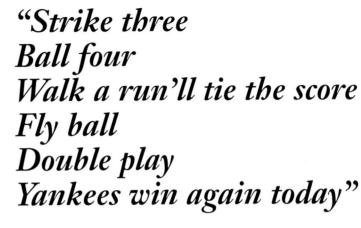

> "*Strike three*
> *Ball four*
> *Walk a run'll tie the score*
> *Fly ball*
> *Double play*
> *Yankees win again today*"
>
> —From the song "Six Months Out of Every Year"
> in *Damn Yankees*

NEW YORK VS. NEW YORK

Next to the Red Sox, Yankee fans most dislike the fellows in orange and blue from Queens. Yankee fans root, root, root for the Mets to lose. The intercity rivalry between the Amazin' Mets and the Bronx Bombers is intense. It has divided families, generated lots of hot air on talk radio, and screamed from tabloid headlines.

It all started innocently enough when the Mets came into existence in 1962. The Yankees and Mets would play the Mayor's Trophy Game, a midseason exhibition that raised funds for youth baseball in the city and also won bragging rights for the winner. Unfortunately, it also instigated bickering between the owners, and the tradition ended in 1983.

Since the advent of interleague play in 1997, there's been no shortage of bickering, bragging, and media hype between the two teams. These Subway Series, played in May and June, take place in a frenzied playoff-like atmosphere.

Never was it more frenzied than in 2000, when the World Series became a Subway Series—the first between two New York teams since Brooklyn lost to the Yankees in 1956. The Yankees won four games to one, but adrenaline was in no short supply. The first Yankees–Mets World Series is forever remembered for Roger Clemens' inexplicable flinging of Mike Piazza's broken bat toward him as he ran to first. As tabloid gossip columnist Cindy Adams liked to say, "Only in New York, kids, only in New York."

A New York baseball fan with divided loyalty

DID YOU KNOW?
YANKEE STADIUM FACTS

The first night game was on May 28, 1946. The Yankees lost to the Washington Senators, 2–1.

Its first electronic message scoreboard debuted in 1959.

The first World Series home run in the Stadium was an inside-the-park job by Casey Stengel of the Giants on October 10, 1923.

Yankee Stadium hosted the 1939, 1960, 1977, and 2008 All-Star Games.

The cost of the 1970s renovation of the Stadium was more than $160 million.

Auxiliary scoreboards were built in the 1940s, covering up the 367-foot right-center sign and 415-foot left-center sign.

The most famous boxing match it ever hosted saw Joe Louis knock out Max Schmeling in the first round on June 22, 1938.

It was home field for football's New York Giants from 1956 to 1973.

The biggest stadium crowd was a Memorial Day doubleheader against Boston on May 30, 1938, with 81,841 in attendance.

A 500-pound beam fell from the upper deck in April 1998, forcing the Yankees to play one home game at Shea Stadium.

Osborn Engineering, which designed Yankee Stadium, also designed Fenway Park and Braves Field in Boston.

BABE BY THE NUMBERS

Major-league career: 1914–1935

Becomes an outfielder: 1918 at age 23

Highest salary in baseball (1930): $80,000

Homers hit in his 20s: 284

Homers hit in his 30s: 424

Homers hit in his 40s: 6

Career home runs: 714

"Boston's greatest baseball player has been cast adrift. George H. Ruth, the middle initial apparently standing for 'HERCULES,' maker of home runs and the most colorful star in the game today, became the property of the New York Yankees."

—JOHN J. HALLAHAN, *BOSTON GLOBE*, JANUARY 6, 1920

MASKED ENEMIES

The Yankees' Thurman Munson was an irritable sort with a squat body. Carlton Fisk of the Red Sox was loquacious, tall, and graceful. About all they had in common was their position (catcher) and a furious dislike for each other.

Their rivalry within the larger team rivalry was sparked by jealousy. Munson always felt that Fisk, who received more votes than him in the 1973 All-Star balloting, had "never been as good a catcher as I am." The tension boiled over on August 1, 1973, when Munson violently collided with Fisk at home plate, triggering a bench-clearing brawl.

So began the first of several notable Red Sox–Yankee donnybrooks in the 1970s. The teams of this era played against each other with fire and aggression, if not downright hatred. In 1976, Graig Nettles body slammed Red Sox lefty Bill Lee to the ground. Lee suffered a shoulder injury that nearly ended his career.

Munson and Fisk collide.

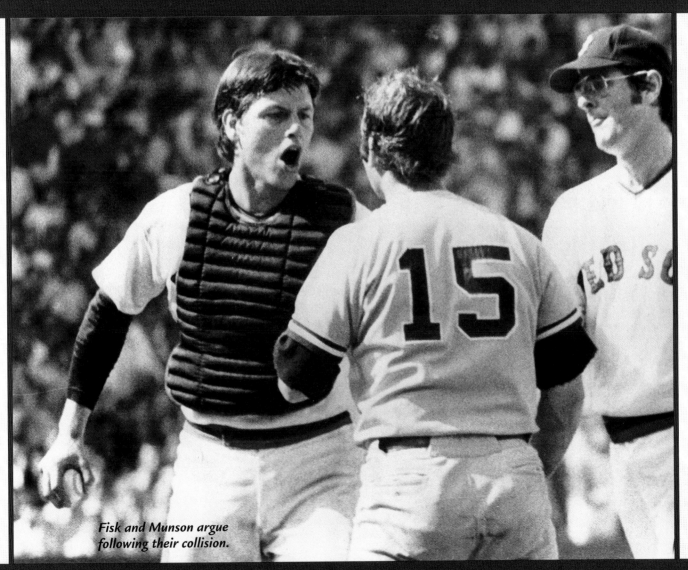

Fisk and Munson argue following their collision.

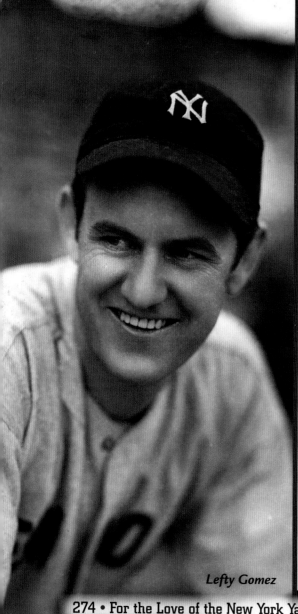

Lefty Gomez

WEARING
THE TRIPLE CROWN

Winning the Triple Crown is a truly elite accomplishment. A player wins the Triple Crown by leading his league in batting average, home runs, and runs batted in. How tough is it? As baseball writer Tim Kurkjian said, "Winning the Triple Crown is so difficult that perhaps there should be an award each season for the player who simply comes closest to doing so."

Only 12 different players have won the batting Triple Crown since the beginning of the 20th century; Rogers Hornsby and Ted Williams each won it twice. The only Yankees to make it were Lou Gehrig (.363, 49, 165) in 1934 and Mickey Mantle (.353, 52, 130) in 1956. Babe Ruth won two legs of the Triple Crown seven times but never led in all three categories.

The pitching Triple Crown—leading the league in wins, strikeouts, and earned run average—is no cakewalk, either. The only Yankee pitcher ever to win the Triple Crown was Lefty Gomez, who did it in 1934 and 1937. In 1934, when Gomez went 26–5 with a 2.33 ERA and 158 strikeouts, he and Gehrig gave the Yankees the distinction of being the only team to ever boast pitching and hitting Triple Crown winners in the same season.

SORROW OF '60

It's still hard to believe that the Yankees lost the 1960 World Series. They outhit the Pittsburgh Pirates (.338 to .256) and outscored them (55 to 27). Despite their best efforts, in Game 7, in the bottom of the ninth, Pittsburgh's light-hitting second baseman, Bill Mazeroski, hit the first-ever World Series-ending home run.

Casey Stengel leaves the field as the Pirates celebrate their Game 7 victory.

YANKEES ABC's

W World Series

No team is as synonymous with the World Series as the Yankees. No team even comes close to the Yankees in terms of World Series appearances. They've played in 39 and won 26.

X X Marks the Spot

Whitey Ford is well known for his incredible control and accuracy on the mound. He finished his career with an amazing 236–106 record. Ford also won a Cy Young Award and appeared in six All-Star Games.

Whitey Ford

Y YES

The Yankee Entertainment and Sports Network, which debuted in 2002, broadcasts the majority of Yankee games. With program offerings such as "Yankee Classics" and "Yankeeography," YES is the prime place to catch the Yankees on TV.

Z Zimmer

The Yankees have had eight players with last names that start with "Z," including the immortal Paul Zuvella, who hit just .122 in parts of two seasons (1986–1987). But their most famous Z-Man is Don Zimmer, the savvy old coach who served as Buddha on the bench during the Yankees' championship years in the late 1990s.

Bobby Murcer was a YES Network broadcaster.

BABE'S BURDEN

Babe Ruth had something to prove in 1923. He'd been suspended for six weeks the previous season for participating in a barnstorming tour, and he hit an embarrassing .118 with no homers in the 1922 World Series. To top it off, he was blistered by the future New York City mayor Jimmy Walker for his beer drinking and boorish behavior. "Will you or not, for the kids of America, solemnly promise to mend your ways?" Walker asked Ruth at an Elks Club dinner. "Will you not give back to those kids their great idol?"

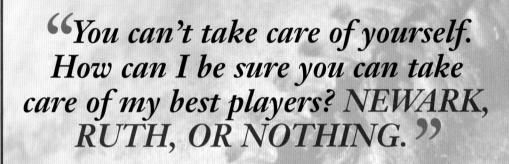

"You can't take care of yourself. How can I be sure you can take care of my best players? NEWARK, RUTH, OR NOTHING."

—YANKEE OWNER JACOB RUPPERT, WHO OFFERED BABE RUTH THE OPPORTUNITY TO MANAGE THE MINOR-LEAGUE NEWARK BEARS IN 1942, BUT NOT THE YANKEES. RUTH CHOSE NOTHING.

MANAGING IN THE CITY

When Joe Torre took over as Yankee manager in 1996, it was the 20th managerial change in the 23 seasons George Steinbrenner had owned the team. He also became the fourth man to manage both the Yankees and Mets. Here's the full list:

MANAGER	YEARS WITH YANKEES	YEARS WITH METS
Casey Stengel	1949–1960	1962–1965
Yogi Berra	1964, 1984–1985	1972–1975
Dallas Green	1989	1993–1996
Joe Torre	1996–2007	1977–1981

Elston Howard and Yogi Berra

BEST YANKEE CATCHERS

Bill Dickey (1928–1943, 1946)
This legendary backstop batted .300 or better 11 times.

Yogi Berra (1946–1963)
Berra was an All-Century selection for catcher (along with Johnny Bench), three-time MVP, and 10-time world champion.

Elston Howard (1955–1967)
A member of nine straight All-Star teams, Howard was 1963 league MVP.

Thurman Munson (1969–1979)
The captain was the heart and soul of 1970s teams.

Jorge Posada (1995–present)
This stellar switch-hitter is making a case for the Hall of Fame.

> ## "I want to thank the Good Lord for making me a YANKEE."
>
> **—JOE DIMAGGIO TO 69,551 FANS WHO GATHERED FOR JOE DIMAGGIO DAY IN 1949**

"If he went 0-for-4 and we lost, he'd sit there in front of his locker for 30, 40 minutes and never move. HE FELT HE'D LET THE CLUB DOWN. No man can carry a club by himself. But that's just the way he felt."

—Eddie Lopat in *Joe DiMaggio—The Golden Year 1941* by Al Silverman

MATTINGLY MATTERS

Don Mattingly may be the best Yankee never to make it to the World Series. Here are some of the impressive numbers from his 14-year career:

Hits: **2,153**
Runs Scored: **1,007**
RBI: **1,099**
Career Batting Average: **.307**

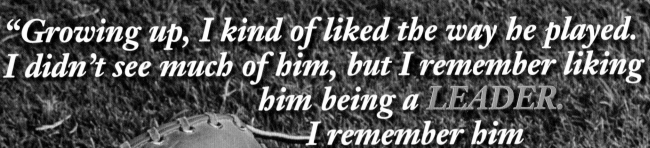

"Growing up, I kind of liked the way he played. I didn't see much of him, but I remember liking him being a *LEADER*. I remember him *STANDING UP FOR HIS TEAMMATES,* and that really caught my eye."

—JORGE POSADA ON THURMAN MUNSON, *THE NEW YORK TIMES, 5/11/04*

INDEX